THE APOSTLE

OF THE CHIPPEWAS

The Life Story of

THE MOST REV. FREDERICK BARAGA, D.D.

the first Bishop of Marquette

By JOSEPH GREGORICH

NIHIL OBSTAT

P. L. BIERMANN

Librorum Censor

IMPRIMATUR

* G. CARDINAL MUNDELEIN, D.D.

Archiepiscopus Chicagienus

January 5, 1935

DEDICATED

TO

MY FATHER

ANTON GREGORICH

AND

TO THE MEMORY OF

MY MOTHER

KATARINA (nee) SIMEC

FROM WHOSE LIPS I FIRST HEARD

THE NAME BARAGA

Bishop Frederic Baraga

Venerable

Born in Slovenia, June 29, 1797

Ordained a Priest, Ljubljana, Slovenia, September 21, 1823

Consecrated Bishop, Cincinnati, Ohio, November 1, 1853

Died in Marquette, Michigan, January 19, 1868

INTRODUCTION TO 2007 EDITION OF
THE APOSTLE OF THE CHIPPEWAS

I have undertaken the preparation of this updated edition of the *Apostle of the Chippewas* written by my father, Joseph Gregorich in 1932, for a number of reasons.

First, I believe it is still the best introduction to the heroic life and challenging times of Bishop Frederic Baraga. His life gives us the example of heroic commitment to God's call through one's vocation. We in the 21st century are not called by God to carry the Gospel to the wilderness and its unbaptized, uncatechized souls. We are all called, however, by reason of our Baptism to bring the Gospel by word or deed to our secular society which has largely abandoned its Christian heritage. This can be intimidating, calling for self-sacrifice and firm commitment. In fulfilling our personal vocation, Bishop Baraga's life is a shining example and encouragement.

Second, I do this to honor my father, Joseph Gregorich (1889-1984), who as a layman devoted a major part of his life and personal resources to making the work and virtue of Bishop Baraga known with the ultimate goal of Baraga's canonization. My father was one of the founders of Bishop Baraga Association which was established in 1930 at St. Stephen Parish in Chicago. While a family man and with a career in engineering he spent his free time researching, documenting and correlating historical data relating to the Bishop from many sources. He traveled to Austria and Communist Yugoslavia to secure and photograph important source materials. His visit to Communist Yugoslavia involved at that time a significant personal risk which never daunted him.

After his retirement he and my mother, Mary, moved to Marquette, Michigan to work full time on the cause. My mother was his partner in their 63 years of marriage as well as his partner in his commitment to Bishop Baraga.

In Marquette, my father spent many years working full time on organizing, translating materials relating to the Cause of Baraga. The collection of historical data on Bishop Baraga which he amassed totals more than six hundred rolls of microfilm and two hundred lineal feet of written material. In 1952, Bishop Thomas Noa, Bishop of Marquette, officially began the Cause for Canonization for Bishop Baraga by submitting to the Congregation of Saints in Rome historical evidences collected and verified by Joseph Gregorich.

Later, the "Position Paper" required by the Congregation, written by Fr. Bruno Korsak, documenting detailed biographical data, providing examples of heroic virtue and evidences of inter-cessary prayer, was also based on the primary historical materials collected by my father. The Congregation accepted this document in 1999, proclaiming Bishop Baraga's life worthy of sainthood and giving him the title "Servant of God."

In publishing this 2007 edition of *The Apostle of the Chippewas*, I am honoring two Slovenian gentlemen, Bishop Frederic Baraga, whom I have considered a saint and loved since my earliest days, and Baraga's historian, Joseph Gregorich, who was my dear father, companion and inspiring role model.

Also very important, this reprinting of *The Apostle of the Chippewas* in 2007 is done as a recognition of the one hundred and fifty year history of the Sault Ste. Marie-Marquette diocese and in tribute to the episcopal and priestly leadership with which the Catholics of this diocese have been blessed through the years.

Any "editing" in the reprinting of this book has been done "gently;" primarily focusing on a few needed corrections. Generally, the 1930's writing style and use of words have been retained. It would not be Joseph Gregorich's writing to do otherwise. The Notes were considered necessary for a more complete understanding of the contents.

I want to express my heartfelt gratitude to Elizabeth Delene, Archivist, Bishop Baraga Association, for her encouragement, assistance and professional guidance throughout this project. Also assisting me in this endeavor have been my friends, Bernadette Kizior and Rita Reichardt whose assistance throughout has been essential to the completion of this edition.

I also thank the Bishop Baraga Association, Chicago Chapter, for reprinting the original copy in 1984, thereby keeping the book's content available through the years.

Pauline Gregorich Scharres

September 2007

CONTENTS

PREFACE

Upon the wild, desolate country in the region of Lake Superior, the Lord cast a sorrowful eye. In His compassion for the many souls living there in misery, in ignorance and in paganism, He sighed for a shepherd who might add this flock to His fold.

Far across the sea He turned that sorrowing eye. Finally, in the land of the Slovenes, where Christian blood had been shed for centuries in battles with the pillaging, ravaging Turks, where the faith was ensanguined by a baptism of blood, there His eyes came to rest upon a castle, permeated with refinement and piety, in which dwelt a soul pure in its baptismal innocence.[1] This soul He nurtured and fashioned by His grace in preparation for the great mission for which He had destined it. Under His hand it flourished until it became His worthy shepherd in this neglected part of the New World. So pleased was He with His first shepherd that He summoned others from the small, pious country of Slovenia, and their noble response has added luster to the history of their people, besides perpetuating gloriously their own names.

The greatest of these newfound shepherds, however, was the first, Frederick Baraga. If his wishes were to be considered, these lines never would be written. So great was his humility that he not only shunned honors but also considered even his deeds unworthy of record. His diary he wrote for himself alone. His soul-baring letters to his sister, Amalia, he did not intend for the prying eyes of the public. Nevertheless, those who come after him cannot be ruled by sentiment. They have a duty to reveal to posterity his essential worth. May this book, which commemorates the one hundredth anniversary of the beginning of his remarkable missionary labors, serve as a worthy tribute to his memory.

The aim of this book is to treat the life of Bishop Baraga in a briefer and more popular form and to refer only to those more outstanding activities of his which possess a greater degree of interest for the general reader. To promote that interest, the book does not always narrate his life chronologically, but, to as great an extent as possible, treats his varied efforts separately.

It is but fitting and proper that the writer acknowledges his debt of gratitude to those who have aided him in preparing this work. The writer feels greatly obliged to three distinguished churchmen who have undertaken to examine and criticize the manuscript: Rt. Rev. Msgr. A. I. Rezek, L.L.D., Rev. J. L. Zaplotnik, J.C.D., V.F., and the Rev. Hugo Bren, S.T.D., O.F.M. Our sincere thanks are also due to Mr. D. Herbert Abel, M.A., of Loyola University, Rev. Philip Gordon, Rev. Oscar Rascher, O.F.M., Rev. F. L. McLaughlin, F. Leonard Bogolin, O.F.M., and Miss Frances Jancer.

If this book helps to stimulate the interest in the lives of our pioneer missionaries, particularly in that of Bishop Baraga, its purpose will have been attained and the work of its compilation more than repaid.

JOSEPH GREGORICH

Chicago, Illinois, October 17, 1931

Note:

1. For several hundred years before Baraga's time, the Balkan's had been invaded numerous time by the Ottoman Turks whose objective was not just the political conquest of the various peoples in these areas, but the conversion, forced if necessary, to Islam. These Turkish armies twice over-run the Balkans reaching the southern outskirts of Vienna in 1529, and in 1683. The second invasion was slightly more than one hundred years before Baraga's birth. Children grew up learning of the horror of these invasions and the heroic responses of their Catholic forebears to these assaults. At the time of Bishop Baraga's birth, the invading Turks were still occupying Bosnia, Serbia, Macedonia,and most of Greece.

CHAPTER I

A Stranger in a Strange Land

On the morning of the last day of the year 1830 a trim, three-masted packet ship arrived at the port of New York. Soon it began to empty its human cargo into the streets of this metropolis of a new world, streets which at the moment, on the day before a holiday, were filled with a hurrying, scurrying humanity.

Among the immigrants who walked down the gangplank was a middle-aged man, rather small of stature but well built, a man who, as a deck passenger, traveling for the lowest fare, was singularly out of place. His bearing was that of a refined and polished gentleman. His expression was one of kindliness and sincerity. His finely moulded features were of a type which bespoke extraordinary character. The broad forehead, firm mouth and well shaped chin indicated a keen intelligence executing its knowledge with determined resolution. Yet, though the name of that ship has been long since forgotten, there is engraved indelibly in history the name of this humble passenger, a saintly missionary, whose life story is nothing, if not a chronicle of noble achievement.

This missionary, Father Frederick Baraga, was the shepherd of the Lord traveling the road to the fields of his new flock, the Indians. He knew that sufferings and privations awaited him. He realized that dangers would arise and that hardships would have to be endured. All these considerations he brushed aside. Within him was the zeal of the self-sacrificing missionary, an indefinable force, that urged him to go "where the harvest is rich and the workers are few." He was accustomed to a life of poverty. His meager personal wants were easily satisfied. His ambition was to bring the light of faith into the lives of the native peoples and to help to dispel for them the darkness of paganism.

Father Baraga had not been always poor. He was, in fact, the scion of an affluent family, the only living son of John Nepomuc Baraga and Katarina (nee) Jencic. Born on June 29, 1797, he was the fourth child out of five to be born to the couple. An older sister, Amalia, and a younger, Antonia, were the only other living children. As the only son, therefore, he was heir apparent to the castle and entire estate at Mala Vas, where he was born.

Mala Vas is within the confines of the parish of Dobrnic, which, at that time, was a part of Lower Carniolia, a province of the Austrian Empire. After World War I, this province was united with others to form Slovenia, which constituted the northwestern part of Yugoslavia.[1] Father Baraga was, therefore, a Slovene by birth and a citizen of the Austrian Empire.

When Frederick was about two years old, his parents sold their possessions at Mala Vas and bought a more pretentious place at Trebnje, two miles distant from Mala Vas and located within the Trebnje parish. At the age of nine, Frederick was sent to Ljubljana to continue his elementary studies under a private tutor. Early in life, he had the misfortune to lose his parents, his mother when he was eleven, and his father four years later.

As partial compensation for this loss, he attracted, by good fortune, the attention of Dr. George Dolinar who, though a layman, was professor of Canon Law in the seminary in Ljubljana. After adopting Frederick as his protege, this learned man guided him in his pursuit of his classical studies at the royal gymnasium. With the advent of the conquering armies of Napoleon, the French language was introduced into the schools, and young Frederick availed himself of the opportunity to learn it, without being conscious of the great advantage that such knowledge would give him in later life.

When he was nineteen years old, in 1816, he entered the University of Vienna to study civil law, in addition to which, by private instruction, he advanced his knowledge of rhetoric, aesthetics, English, French, Italian and Spanish.[2] As an unusually bright and obedient scholar, he acquitted himself well in all his studies, but was especially apt in languages. He was always neat in appearance, took good care of his health, and shunned alcoholic liquors. Although his chief diversion was painting, he enjoyed also long recreational walks, particularly during vacation time. Among these were some long hiking trips by which he unknowingly prepared himself for the many fatiguing journeys that awaited him in the fulfillment of his life's work.

Notes:
1. In 1991, Slovenia declared its independence from Yugoslavia and is now a member of the European Union.
2. Vienna was the capital of the Austrian Empire which at Baraga's time included, Bohemia, Bulgaria, Hungary, part of Poland, Romania, Slovakia and Slovenia. In addition to being the political center, it was the cultural and educational center for the entire Empire. Education in any of the professions was based in Vienna.

CHAPTER II

The Saintly Youth

Gifted by nature and endowed with worldly goods, he might have satisfied his temporal wants and lived in ease, an honored lord and master on his large estate. Baraga, however, did not care for riches, ease or honors. Nor did he seek worldly happiness. In his young heart were sober, manly, noble thoughts, nurtured in an environment productive of a saintly life.

Young Frederick had the priceless blessing of being born of God-fearing, Christian parents into a home of culture, of innate refinement and of charity. From his early childhood, his parents instilled into his heart the love of God, and taught him to be charitable to the poor. Priestly tutors guided his early education, and later, their instruction was supplemented by the wisdom of the distinguished and pious scholar, Dr. Dolinar.

In Vienna, a city of many temptations, a kind Providence placed him under the spiritual guidance of a noted confessor and preacher, Saint Clement Maria Hofbauer.[1] The influence of this saintly man had a salutary effect on the sensitive youth, who imbibed Saint Clement's zeal and unconsciously fashioned his life after so noble a pattern.

At the time of his entrance into the university, Frederick was engaged to be married to the daughter of his friend and guardian, Dr. Dolinar, who had fond visions of the happy union of his child and protege. As the young student's breadth of intellect increased, however, his strength of conviction in a religious vocation began to grow. He became more reserved, more serious-minded. One of his comrades, in fact, noticing this change in Frederick's interests, remarked in jest that Anna, his fiancee, would never be his wife. Frederick vowed that, after a year, he would marry her. However, a short time later, God's call began to assert itself, and during his last year at the university, he made a sudden but a firm decision to espouse Holy Orders. His decision was the product only of much deliberation. Nonetheless, it surprised his relatives and friends, since Baraga had confided his secret to no one until he felt satisfied that he was fitted for the vocation that he was about to choose. The fact that he loved and respected his benefactor, Dr. Dolinar, to whom he felt much indebted, made his decision difficult indeed. Later it was recalled that he referred often to a painting of the Good Shepherd, which had come from under his brush, and through which possibly God had made known to him His call. It is also reasonable to suppose that Frederick had consulted his saintly confessor, Saint Clement, whose encouragement and prayers undoubtedly influenced his decision.

In the autumn of 1821, after being graduated from law school, he entered the diocesan seminary in Ljubljana. After two years of close application and exemplary conduct, during which time Baraga completed the regular three-year course, he was ready for Holy Orders. On September 21, 1823, the day of his ordination, he consecrated his life to the service of his Divine Master, and in the cathedral, on the following day, he celebrated his first Mass. On entering the seminary, he had severed his last worldly ties by waiving all claims to his inheritance in favor of his sister, Amalia, and now he refused even a small annuity of six hundred florins that his sister urged him to accept.

Notes:
    1. St. Clement Maria Hofbauer (1751-1830) was a Redemptorist priest, teacher and reformer.
    After the suppression of religious institutions during the Napoleonic era, St. Clement worked to reestablish, rebuild Catholic schools, colleges and other institutions to revitalize the Catholic Faith in Austria. He was known for his holiness and zeal especially among the young.

CHAPTER III

The Zealous Curate

After continuing his studies for another year, young Father Baraga was assigned to Saint Martin's parish, in Upper Carniolia, as an assistant priest. From the very beginning of his labors as curate, his zeal and ability were evidenced by better attendance at the services and by an increase in the frequency of reception of the Sacraments. He applied himself so unceasingly and with such unremitting energy that his sister felt obliged to warn him not to undermine his health. For him, nevertheless, his work was nour-

ishment in itself, for he thrived physically in spite of the exhaust-
ing pace he was setting for himself.

Here he began to accustom himself to the privations and
hardships that seemed preordained for him. He chastened his
body by fasting and by sleeping on boards covered with a little
straw. Often his meals consisted of only bread and water. He seldom ate meat, and seldom drank liquor.

His tactfulness in the confessional made that Sacrament
more popular. After instilling a fear of God's eternal justice, he
would refresh the penitent by his explanation of the infinite foun-
tain of mercy that springs from the Same Source. With kind but
firm admonitions to fortify his sympathetic advice, he eased the
hearts of sinners while guiding them back to the road of salvation.
His sermons attracted hosts of people, since few could preach with
his sincerity and depth of feeling. His resonant, well modulated,
rich, low voice carried a power of conviction that stirred the hearts
of the most hardened sinners.

The parishioners loved and revered Father Baraga for his
many acts of kindness and charity. He was known to have given
his shoes to a poor, barefoot traveler whom he had met while on
an errand of mercy. He had sheltered and had nursed back to
health a stranger whom he had found lying, sick and helpless,
beside a road. Even in these early years, this kind, pious and zeal-
ous priest was regarded by many as a living saint.

The country at the time was in the throes of Jansenism, or,
as it was called in Austria, Josephinism, the secular interference
and state supremacy in ecclesiastical affairs. Their adherents made
the reception of the Sacraments difficult and infrequent. They
banned sodalities and pilgrimages and lessened the frequency and

splendor of services, particularly the exposition and veneration of the Blessed Sacrament. Father Baraga, on the other hand, attracted many to the Sacraments. He filled the church with a pious throng and formed sodalities. His heavenly minded activities met with opposition and his resulting popularity created a jealousy and ill-will among some of his colleagues which, after four years, resulted in his transfer as curate to the neglected parish of Metlika, near the border of Croatia.

With unabated devotion to duty, he continued his efforts in this spiritually hungry community until, by his tireless activities and his sterling talents and ability, he had created there a new appreciation of religious living. In a short time, the Sunday afternoon services were well attended by the people, eager to hear his clear explanations of the Christian Doctrine. As early as two or three o'clock on Sunday morning the cook would inform Father Baraga that people, some of whom came from afar, were waiting at his confessional. He taught those children to read and write whose parents were too poor to send them to school. Shortly after his arrival, he managed to provide the much needed Stations of the Cross, and with great solemnity he hung them in place with his own hands. Finally, the altar was renovated. New vestments were bought and certain necessary repairs were made to the church. Nearly all these improvements were financed by his sister's monetary gifts to him.

CHAPTER IV

"Where the Harvest Is Rich and the Workers Are Few"

Young Father Baraga never was idle. When he was not engaged in his pastoral duties, he occupied himself with literary work. During the early years of his priesthood he translated some books into Slovene, besides composing several others in the same tongue. Among these was his crowning work, a prayer book, entitled *Pasture for the Soul* (Dusna Pasa), a devotional collection of prayers which proved very suitable for the needs of his people and which satisfied a long-felt[1] want. This book, regarded by Slovenes as a precious souvenir of his memory, has retained its popularity even in this modern day. It has been reprinted at least ten times, and the last edition, that of 1905, numbered about eighty-five thousand copies. If one considers the fact that there are only about one and three-quarter million Slovenes in all the world, one must conclude that a book must enjoy unquestioned popularity to warrant the publication of so large an edition. Recently, too, an edition appeared translated into German.

In 1829, the Leopoldine Society was organized in Vienna for the purpose of promoting the foundation and the support of the American Indian and other missions.[2] The news of this society's beginning opened the way to a realization of the secret desire of Father Baraga to become a missionary, since the illwill of his colleagues harassed him even in remote Metlika. He obtained permission to undertake American missionary work upon the condition that he first be accepted in some American diocese. With this purpose in view, he wrote to Bishop Fenwick of Cincinnati on November 13, 1829.[3] He received no reply. For a time he doubted whether God had intended him for missionary work, but later he considered the possibility of his letter being lost, and accordingly, he wrote again on April 5, 1830. To this letter came the answer that brought genuine joy to his heart. He was readily accepted, and, because of the scarcity of priests, he was urged to come with all haste.

One Sunday, after the regular afternoon service, he gave a brief farewell address. The people were grieved. Many wept. As he left the church, scores of them followed him and kissed his cloak. On the next day, entirely composed, he boarded a stage-coach that waited to take him away. Unable to control themselves, the parishioners cried out, hanging on the reins of the horses and to the wheels of the coach, and begged him to bless them again in parting. This touching tribute, however, angered the pastor, prompting him to say maliciously:

"You brought here new fangled notions and incurred debts for your own aggrandizement. Who will pay for that now?" "You know that my pockets are empty," Father Baraga answered sadly, "but I will gladly leave my overcoat to help pay any debts." This was a new coat that he had bought for the trip to conceal his old, worn clothes underneath.

The mild reproof of the curate incited the people against the pastor, who was forced to flee for his safety without even the solace of Father Baraga's overcoat. Thus, revered by his parishoners but hated by some of his colleagues, Father Baraga practically was compelled to leave his native land that he might, with his characteristic zeal, labor unrestrictedly for God.

Thus, revered by his parishioners but hated by some of his colleagues, Father Baraga practically was compelled to leave his native land that he might, with his characteristic zeal, labor unrestrictedly for God.

After stopping at Ljubljana, the capital of Slovenia, he continued his journey on October 29, aboard a stagecoach bound for Vienna. Upon his arrival in the Austrian capital he was cordially received by the Leopoldine Society. He was given presents and his passage for America, and, on December 1, 1830, he sailed from Havre, France, for the New World, where he was to earn for himself undying fame and a place near the throne of his Master.

Notes:
1. Father Baraga's book, Dusna Pasa, *Pasture for the Soul* was never published in English. It was written for the "general public" rather than the "elite or privileged" which was custom at that time. Father Baraga's other book published (1830) in Slovene was *Veneration and Intimidation of the Blessed Mother of God*.
2. Leopoldine Society was founded in Austria in 1829, in response to the growing interest in foreign missions which developed after the Propagation of Faith was founded in Paris in 1822 to support French missionaries. The emperor and other members of the royal family were instrumental in founding the society. It was named "Leopoldine Society" to perpetuate the memory of Leopoldian, a favorite daughter of Francis I, the Austrian Emperor at that time. The beneficiaries of the society were principally missionaries in the United States. The first funds were sent to Bishop Fenwick in Cincinnati.
3. Bishop Dominic Fenwick, a Dominican Priest (1768-1832), was born in St. Mary's County, Maryland. He was consecrated the first bishop of Cincinnati in 1822. At the time of its establishment the diocese of Cincinnati included what was then known as the "Northwest Territory." This area covered what is now the states of Ohio, Michigan, Indiana, Illinois and Wisconsin. After Bishop Fenwick's death in 1832, other dioceses in the area began to be established, the first being the diocese of Detroit.

CHAPTER V

On His Way to the Indians

That fatiguing month aboard ship which included episodes of seasickness during the stormy voyage compelled Father Baraga to rest for a few days upon reaching New York. In this city of two hundred thousand population he learned that only four churches out of one hundred and sixty were Catholic. This small number of tabernacles did not seem to him to be a very encouraging sign of a flourishing condition of the Church in the New World. It must be remembered, however, that only about forty years before, a Catholic priest was subject to the death penalty, if, of his own volition, he entered the State of New York, a circumstance not calculated to give an impetus to the founding of churches.[1]

After five days in New York Father Baraga went to Philadelphia, where he preached in German his first sermon on American soil. After he had paid his respects to the Archbishop of Baltimore, he started by stagecoach for Cincinnati. His first exposure to danger in the New World occurred during this trip. He narrowly escaped serious injury and possible death when the horses became frightened and ran away. Fortunately for the riders, the stagecoach was unoccupied at the time of the accident, while Father Baraga and his fellow passengers were warming themselves and resting at an inn. The horses were killed. The coach, tuning over into a ravine, was wrecked completely. Thus, at the outset of his journey into the wilderness, Divine Providence had shown special care for him, protecting and preserving him for the distinctive service he was to perform.

He arrived in Cincinnati on January 18, 1831. Bishop Fenwick, besides expressing pleasant surprise at Father Baraga's arrival in his warm greeting to him, was elated at the missionary's sincere desire and impatient eagerness to begin his labors among the Indians. The bishop had intended him for a mission post in Michigan, but travel to the north at that time of the year was out of the question. Father Baraga, accordingly, busied himself with pastoral work, while perfecting himself in English, in addition to mastering the strange-sounding, and difficult language of the Indians. His tutor in the Indian tongue was an eighteen-year-old, full-blooded Ottawa Indian, a student at the seminary where Father Baraga stayed.

In the spring, Fr. Baraga left Cincinnati for Dayton, Ohio. While on his way there, he performed missionary work, beginning at Miamisburg, Ohio. To his sorrow, he found so many lukewarm Catholics and unbelievers that, for a time, he was undecided whether to remain there, where he found such a rich field for his zeal, or to go farther. In the end, though, he was assured that the prospect of fruitful work was better among the Indians, and that the need of his services there was even greater.

In Dayton, he was joined by his bishop and from there he accompanied him to Mackinac, where they visited Father Mazzuchelli.[2] On May 28, when they arrived at Arbre Croche, the Indians were happy to see their bishop and to learn that Father Baraga was to remain among them.[3] On the feast of Corpus Christi, Bishop Fenwick said Mass, which was followed by a procession with the Blessed Sacrament. The piety, dignity and devotion displayed by the natives on this occasion deeply affected the prelate. Such a pious sight seldom was to be seen even in highly civilized countries.

"Happy day," Father Baraga wrote to his sister on June 10, 1831, "that placed me among the Indians, with whom I will now remain uninterruptedly to the last breath of my life." So began Father Baraga's thirty-seven years of illustrious missionary labors, for, although he died a bishop, he remained to the end a missionary to the Indians.

Notes:
1. Before becoming a part of the New United States in 1783, New York was a English Colony. In the 1500's England had instituted severe anti-Catholic laws and penalties which were also applied in the English colonies. These laws did not apply once New York became part of the new United States, however significant. anti-Catholic prejudice continued. England itself repealed these anti-Catholic laws in 1829.
2. Samuel Mazzuchelli O.P., now Venerable, was born of a wealthy family of merchants and bankers in Milan, Italy in 1806. At age 17, against his father's wishes, he entered the Order of Preaches (Dominican Order). At the age of 22 he came to Cincinnati. Bishop Fenwick assigned Father Mazzuchelli to be a missionary priest to the whole of the Northwest Territory. In 1847, Father Mazzuchelli founded, with two women, the Sinsinawa Dominican Congregation. He died in 1864.
3. Arbre Croche (Crooked Tree) is located near present day Harbor Springs, Michigan.

CHAPTER VI

The Indians Around the Upper Great Lakes

Before narrating further the life of Father Baraga among the Indians, let us glance back into the history of the American Indians, in order that we may appreciate better the conditions under which he labored.

Many years before his coming, the Indians were a warlike, superstitious, unmoral people, who invoked the rivers, the lakes and the moon as some of their gods, or, as they called them, their manitous. Various objects also served as idols, which they worshiped. Absurd legends were told of spirits that were supposed to people the land, the sea and the sky. These manitous, idols and legends comprised the Indian's answer to his soul's craving for a recognition of the true God, a craving which the natives could not interpret correctly, steeped as they were in the ignorance of paganism.

The French Jesuit Fathers, the first to bring Christianity to the Lake Superior regions, came here in the seventeenth century and suffered untold hardships, cruelties, humiliations and even martyrdom for their faith.[1] With undaunted perseverance they cultivated the goodwill of the Indians, patiently bearing insults and maltreatment, and finally earning their respect and love. Among those who labored here was St. Isaac Jogues, who fell victim to a treacherous Iroquois tomahawk in New York state, and who was canonized in 1930; Father Allouez, who established many missions in his quarter of a century of labors; and Father Jacques Marquette, the intrepid explorer of the Mississippi River Valley.

Missionary activities in this section practically ceased in the eighteenth century due to the four long wars which unsettled the lives of the Indians and suppressed the labors of the Society of Jesus. Many of the Indians reverted to their former lives. It was not, in fact, until the close of the War of 1812 that peace again reigned over this region.

In the first part of the nineteenth century, however, Indians were not the cruel, wild natives nor did they skulk in the brush at the coming of a white man. They were, of a certainty, proud and haughty, but docile withal, for they had fought, had been defeated and subdued, and had been forced to acknowledge the permanent presence of the white race. Although there were many bands roving in the forests, still, some of the groups had a fixed place of habitation, where, because a spark of faith had remained in them, they yearned for a "black-robe," a name they used for a priest.

One of the first of such Indian settlements to have a resident priest was Arbre Croche. Father Dejean had come to this place some two years before the advent of Father Baraga. During his time there he baptized about two hundred natives, and built a church, a school and a parsonage, all made of logs and having a roof of birch bark. These buildings, crude as they were, entailed much labor. Practically the only tool at hand was an ax. The big, heavy logs had to be carried on the shoulders of the Indians, since no other form of transportation was available.

About six months before the arrival of Father Baraga, Father Dejean was forced to abandon his successful missionary work, as his personal affairs demanded his presence in his native France.

Note:

    1. The Jesuits were members of the Society of Jesus, a religious order founded by St. Ignatius of Loyola and approved by Pope Paul III in 1540. In 1641, the first Jesuits, including St. Isaac Jogues arrived in Sault Ste. Marie, Michigan. The first chapel was built in 1668. Father Jacques Marquette was assigned to Sault Ste. Marie. St. Mary's parish in Sault Ste. Marie is the third oldest parish in the United States.

CHAPTER VII

The Beginning of His Missionary Labors

The migratory Ottawa Indian village of Waganakisi, or Arbre Croche (Crooked Tree), later named Little Traverse, occupied in Baraga's time, the present site of Harbor Springs, Emmet County, near the northern end of Lower Michigan.

Here Father Baraga began his labors, and proved, from the very beginning thereof, his fitness as a missionary. His industry, piety, humility and sincerity won many new converts to the faith and soon earned him the love and respect of the Indians, who affectionately called him Father. Within two and a half months he had baptized seventy, and, before the year 1831 had passed, he had increased this number to one hundred and thirty-one.

Through an interpreter, a French-speaking, full-blooded Ottawa Indian of good repute, he preached, heard confessions and sometimes taught school. Accompanied by this faithful Indian, Father Baraga went from wigwam to wigwam, visiting the

Christian Indians and seeking to convert the others. He wrote of the "undescribable joy and consolation" that he experienced when administering Baptism. In a letter to the Leopoldine Society under the date of August 22, 1831, he spoke of "a happy, never-to-be-forgotten day, for I have baptized at one time eleven Indians," although on many later occasions he baptized even greater numbers at a time.

Sometimes a non-Christian Indian would bring to him his idols and other articles which excited the superstitious nature of the Indian, requesting that Father Baraga burn them in token of the native's willingness to embrace Christianity. The missionary would participate gladly in such ceremonious offerings, and, as the smoke from the fire, which was destroying these symbols of paganism, rose heavenward, he would pray "that the God of hosts, who alone should be adored, receive with pleasure this sacrifice."

His burning zeal transformed Arbre Croche into a model Christian community. On Sundays and Holy days of obligation there were three other services besides Mass, whereas on weekdays, Mass and morning and evening services were held, all of which were well attended. He heard confessions almost every day, sometimes to the number of twenty or thirty. During the week between Christmas and New Year's Day, to his great satisfaction, the entire village received the Sacraments.

When Bishop Fenwick again visited Arbre Croche, during the following summer, Father Baraga's diligent preparations gave his Excellency a pompous welcome. They all knelt for his blessing and manifested genuine joy at his coming by firing a rifle salute in his honor. The bishop, deeply touched, imparted to them his blessing and shook their hands, for he considered them the pride of his diocese.

After being with the Indians a little over a year, Father Baraga had mastered their language sufficiently to compose, in the Ottawa tongue, a prayer book and hymnal. But it was only by denying himself much needed rest that he was able to prepare this work, the first of a series of his notable contributions to Native American literature.

Surely nothing but his missionary zeal made his life bearable in this forlorn, inhospitable place. His log house was but a hut, hardly a fit place in which to live. Throughout the long, cold winter the winds blew their chilly blasts through the many crevices. In summer the rain dripped through a roof of birch bark that afforded but little protection. To keep his bed dry he spread his umbrella over it. His books and table he covered with his cloak. He himself sat down wherever he could find a dry spot. He lived meagerly, fasted often, prayed much and worked untiringly. Although this highly educated and refined man lived a life bare of the comforts of civilization, separated from friends and native land, he never uttered a word of complaint. Rather, he thanked God warmly for the privilege of thus serving Him. In a letter to his sister, Amalia, dated March 10, 1832, he wrote, "It is unspeakably joyful and consoling to me to be here . . . . I cannot sufficiently thank God for my coming here where so much good can be done."

CHAPTER VIII

He Blesses His First Church

Everywhere the conduct of Father Baraga's Christianized Indians commended itself to the observant eyes of non-Christian Indians. Therefore, he was invited to visit other settlements which were well disposed toward Christianity. In that vast Upper Michigan territory, an area of a radius of several hundred miles, there was but one other priest. Father Baraga deplored this lack of missionaries, for he realized keenly how limited were his own powers. The thought of the great number of souls uncared for lay heavily on his heart.

Since, by the following spring, nearly all the Indians in the vicinity of Arbre Croche had been baptized, he became restless. To appease his missionary longings, he decided to visit some of the more distant settlements. Now he began those trying and perilous missionary journeys that were to test severely his endurance, his courage and his trust in God.

His first objective was Beaver Island, the largest of an insular group at the northern end of Lake Michigan. Not without fear did he and his companions approach the island, for they were not certain of the nature of their reception. Nevertheless, the chief and his people bade the "black-robe" and his wayfarers a friendly welcome to their poor village. After several visits to the island, Father Baraga succeeded in converting fifty-five, but the hostility of the others prevented him from establishing there a permanent mission.

On the opposite shore of the lake, at Manistique, he encountered a settlement which, though smaller than Beaver Island, was more inclined to listen to his teachings. Advised of his coming, the Indians began to build a church of logs and bark, which he and his companions completed on the day they arrived. The next morning the missionary and his curious band of worshipers gathered around this hut in the wilderness where, only a short time before, pagan worship had held unchallenged sway. Dressed in his priestly vestments, Father Baraga began the Holy Rite, while the natives stared at the simple, quiet ceremony so strange to them. The rustling of the leaves murmured an answer to his prayers, and a choir of birds sang a paean of Thanksgiving to their Creator, as the priest, with all the solemnity befitting the consecration of a cathedral, dedicated this humble edifice, his first church, to the honor of the Blessed Mother of God, thus fulfilling to her his promise made while yet in his native land. Tears came to his eyes as he thought that, not long ago, the beating of drums had called these children of nature to their pagan ceremonies, whereas now God Himself deigned to live among them in this modest abode.

In time, Father Baraga christened this entire village of nineteen natives with the sole exception of one stubborn old man. He praised repeatedly the piety of these Indians and marveled at their tenacious hold on their faith, for, even though his visits to them were few and infrequent, they would gather in their rough-hewn church, sometimes as often as two or three times a day, to recite the rosary and to sing hymns.

In a frail, unseaworthy boat, and with the weather unfavorable, he crossed the lake on a venturesome missionary journey to Little Detroit Island, in the spring of 1833.[1] As the skimpy craft was tossed unmercifully on the rough waves, it seemed as if at any moment it would be dashed to pieces. The lake gushed over the sides. It threatened to swallow the small craft, but Father Baraga, entirely self-composed and with supreme confidence in his Master's protection, calmly encouraged the men accompanying him. When, after a miserable and perilous journey, they arrived safely at their destination, they were more than repaid for the hardships they had suffered by the warm welcome which they received and the ultimate conversions which they made among the islanders.

In the winter this missionary traveled upon heavy and cumbersome snowshoes. In the summer he braved the dangers of the lake. Untiringly he labored on. Nothing could swerve him from his course. During his two years and four months of fruitful labors at Arbre Croche and in its vicinity, this shepherd had brought four hundred and eighty-one souls to the fold of his Master. Yet, notwithstanding the fact that his fame as a missionary had already spread far and wide, had penetrated the wilderness and had spanned the shores of the lake, his success, far from making him proud, seemed but to increase his humility. As Father Haetscher has written, "He works miracles of salvation. He is very poor, lives like a Trappist, but with all that prizes himself overhappy."[2] These are the qualities for which he was loved by the natives, who appreciated his modesty as well as his greatness.

Notes:

1. Little Detroit Island is located in Lake Michigan, off the Door County Peninsula, Wisconsin.
2. Father Francis Haetscher, born in Vienna in 1784, was spiritually mentored, as was Federic Baraga, by St. Clement Hofbauer. He was ordained a Redemptorist priest in 1816. He began his missionary activites in the United States in 1832. He worked among the Menominee Indians in Green Bay, Wisconsin and later was sent to Mackinaw Island and to Sault Ste. Marie. He returned to Europe in 1838.

CHAPTER IX

He Establishes a Mission at Grand River

"Happy news, my Father, happy news!" This pleasant greeting came from an Indian who, at the request of Father Baraga, had played the role of Saint John the Baptist by preparing the way for him among the Ottawas at Grand River, a settlement about two hundred miles south of Arbre Croche.[1] This pious Indian had performed his task faithfully and well, and reported that the natives at that settlement would be pleased to see and hear the "envoy of the Great Spirit."

That same spring, June 7, 1833, he started on the long journey to Grand River, stopping at the present site of the city of Grand Rapids. A French Canadian family offered him shelter and granted him the use of a portion of a practically new house as a temporary church. This good, Catholic family was happy to see Father Baraga, for he was the first priest to come to that beautiful country in many a year.

The Indians, many of whom had never seen a "black-robe," came and listened with marked attention to the truths of Christianity, explained in their own native tongue. In three weeks' time he had converted eighty-six Indians. His success convinced the bishop that a permanent congregation at this spot was a necessity, not only for the Indians already converted but also for the many white Catholics living in the vicinity. At his own request, Father Baraga, who in the meantime had returned to Arbre Croche, was charged with the task.

A successor was appointed for his post in Arbre Croche, and soon thereafter he was on his way again to Grand River. Although he regretted leaving his good and pious Indians at Arbre Croche, the thought of starting his own mission and of the greater opportunities for conversions roused his missionary zeal and stifled his sentimental feelings. Opportunely, he received a box of religious articles and a sum of money from a group of his benefactors in his native Slovenia. He felt very grateful for these gifts, since he deemed them so very necessary for the success of his new mission.

It was September 8, 1833, when he left Arbre Croche permanently for his new mission post at Grand River. Immediately upon his arrival, thirteen days later, he assembled the Indians and announced his intention to remain and to build a church and a school. The Catholic Indians were very well pleased. Of the others, some seemed unconcerned and a small number strenuously objected. These objectors were the converts of a Protestant missionary, a man who, though well financed, had succeeded in converting but ten in about nine years. Father Baraga had converted eighty-six in three weeks. Incited by jealousy, these Protestant Indians endeavored to prevent Father Baraga from settling there and building a church. Since their unreasonable objections made it evident to all that their actions were prompted solely by bigotry, the majority of the natives warmly approved Father Baraga's stand on his rights. The objectors, ashamed, yielded and left the assembly.

The building of the church and the school was beset with many difficulties. After a vain search for skilled mechanics in the vicinity, the missionary was forced finally to undertake a fatiguing journey to Detroit in quest of help. When winter came on, the progress of the construction was slowed up, while his expenditures for material, wages and food for his help were fast depleting his funds.

Without a church his mission would undoubtedly fail. But where could he, so poor a man, among even poorer people, get the means to pay for it? "With outstretched hands, I beg you to have compassion on your unfortunate brothers in this part of the world," he wrote imploringly to the Leopoldine Society, his benefactors in the past. And his pleas were not in vain.

Note:
1. Grand River is the present day Grand Rapids, Michigan.

CHAPTER X

Surrounded by Wickedness

Throughout these early days at Grand River he lived in a miserable hovel, which he described as resembling an open milk shed, so little protection from the winter weather did it afford. His surroundings, a composite of drunkenness, wickedness, superstition and paganism, were far from agreeable. To a sensitive saintly nature, such as his was, all this squalor and irreligion was repulsive, detestable and sacrilegious. Nevertheless, he bore all these trials with a fortitude prompted by a heavenly hope.

"Were it not," he wrote, "for the ardent desire and fond hope I cherish that some unhappy soul now groping in the darkness of paganism, which leads to perdition, will be saved, nothing in this world could induce me to remain here. . ."

In the spring of 1834 came the long-awaited day, April 20, on which the church was to be dedicated. Although the structure was unfinished and crude in appearance, the inside was ornamented richly with pictures and religious articles sent to him by his friends in Europe. Led by an Indian carrying a cross, the small, solemn procession marched to the church. Reverently, Father Baraga dedicated it in honor of the Blessed Virgin. This rare ceremony, especially in a setting so primitive, was witnessed by many non-Catholics, both white and red.

Father Baraga had one archenemy against whom he had to fight with all his might — whiskey. White traders, with little honesty but with plenty of "fire-water," demoralized the Indians, who, as a rule, had an almost unquenchable thirst for strong liquor. Wherever these traders went, debauchery and revelry stalked after them. After getting the Indians in a drunken stupor, they would bargain for the native's furs. Often whiskey was traded for furs, a practice that brought starvation and misery to the Indian's family. When drunk, an Indian would become a terrifying creature. His pent-up warlike nature would seem to have been released. The native men, when in that condition, have been known to commit murder, the women to bite off each other's noses, ears and fingers.

Father Baraga's pleas and admonitions to the traders were to no avail. They were answered with insults and threats. In malice, they brought more whiskey to the Indians. Because they feared his influence, they slandered him and belittled his teachings. He had taught the Indians to cultivate their lands and to live a settled life. The traders, however, were unwilling to have the natives abandon their hunting and their nomadic life, for they were interested, not in the welfare of the Indian, but in the value of his furs.

On one occasion, when a trader had brought a large quantity of liquor into the village, the Indians were on a continuous drunken spree for four days. During that time Father Baraga almost lost his life. A drunken and warlike mob, incited and instigated against him, had made its way toward his cabin. Warned by their wild yells, he bolted his door and windows just in time. They surrounded his cabin and tried to effect an entrance, but were too drunk to succeed. For a time, he thought that his cabin would be his funeral pyre, for he feared that they would set it ablaze. Kneeling in the center of the room, he prayed calmly and fervently, vowing that, if he were spared, he would observe total abstinence from liquor for the remainder of his life. Trustingly he placed his life in the hands of the One who can subdue the most irresponsible mobs. For four hours they howled around his cabin. Help came at last. The Indians were dispersed; and by the grace of God he was spared.

CHAPTER XI

His Influence Causes His Removal

In spite of many discouragements, Father Baraga contin-ued his labors, uncomplaining. He found conversions in Grand River more difficult. The Indians were more demoralized and more seriously addicted to vice than those at Arbre Croche. However, his life was not barren of sunshine. With great satisfac-tion he noted that on Christmas Day nearly all the natives came to Mass and received the Sacraments. Some came from afar, a dis-tance of three or four days' travel. Among them were venerable old men and women, some of whom were weak and sickly. Not a few were mere children. These former pagans were now becoming Christian heroes who, by their piety and their loyalty to the faith, were giving convincing evidence of his greatness as a missionary.

Among his converts was a noted chief, a brave warrior who, when drunk, had terrified all who came near. After his con-version this bold warrior abstained from liquor and became a good Christian. He worked, prayed and exhorted others to abandon paganism. The howling wolf had been transformed into a meek, Christian lamb.

When Father Baraga was in Muskegon at one of his mis-sions, a seventeen year-old Indian girl begged him to baptize her. She had come, quite some distance, against the wishes of her pagan father, who had threatened to cut off her ears if she should become a Christian. Notwithstanding her father's threat, she was sincere in her intentions, and, after some instructions, she was baptized. Happy in her newfound grace, she left for home with strength to meet courageously whatever fate awaited her.

The great distance between camps and settlements increased the difficulties of his missionary labors. Father Baraga was obliged to penetrate the dense virgin forests clogged with heavy undergrowth, to plod through the swamps and bogs that, in the summer time, swarmed with mosquitoes, to wade across rivers or to risk his life on an unsteady log, that served as a bridge over raging, speeding waters. But for all the hardships that he endured he would consider himself well repaid by the unfeigned joy that the Indians always displayed upon his arrival.

While his success as a missionary was increasing the hatred and bitterness of the traders in Grand River, there loomed now on the horizon other enemies, foes much more powerful, who were playing for higher stakes than pelts. These were the land grabbers who coveted the Indians' lands. The unschooled, trusting natives too often became the prey of an Indian agent who had the duty of protecting them. After giving them an insignificant sum of money for their valuable lands, the agent would often deport them westward, like so many cattle, to their new reservations.

When rumors arose that the Indian lands around Grand River were to be sold, the Ottawas convened a Grand Council, witnessed by Father Baraga, at which they expressed their intention of retaining their lands. But, despite their resolution, the Indian agent was ordered to secure their signature to a release of their possessions. Soon it became apparent that the Indian agent would fail in this task as long as the Indians remained under the moral influence of Father Baraga. His keen sense of justice would not permit him to remain silent should anyone want to take advantage of them. For this reason the speculators were determined that he be removed.

At their instigation, Father Baraga was accused by the Indian agent of being the cause of Indian disturbances. This charge, however, was dismissed when Father Baraga's conduct was upheld by the Governor of Michigan. At length, unknown to the missionary, pressure was brought to bear upon Bishop Rese to effect his removal, and, in order to keep peace with the government officials against whom he was powerless, the bishop agreed to the demand.[1] In reality, this incident is a genuine tribute to a humble missionary, whose power over the Indians earned for him the notice of the government.

Father Baraga made but little mention of this occurrence. His feelings were deeply hurt, and it was with sorrow and reluctance that he left his beloved Ottawas. The fact that he made no complaint proved his real greatness, for he realized that his bishop could not have acted otherwise.

Note:
1. Bishop Rese was the Bishop of the newly founded Diocese of Detroit, Michigan, in which Grand Rapids was located.

CHAPTER XII

He Comes to the Chippewas

During the winter of 1834-1835, which he spent at a French mission at Saint Claire, near Detroit, he wrote to his sister, Amalia, on March 13, that here he felt "like a fish on dry land" after being so long among the Indians. While at Saint Claire he received another box of religious articles. The gift was a very welcome one, since it was precisely what he needed for the mission he was about to re-establish.

With the opening of navigation on the lakes, on June 8, he left Detroit for his new mission post, some six hundred miles away. When the boat stopped at Mackinac, he availed himself of the opportunity to visit Arbre Croche. His joy in seeing his former parishioners was tempered by the sad news that they were at that time without a priest. The Indians begged their beloved missionary to remain with them, but he told them regretfully that duty compelled him to go to those who needed him more. With a heavy heart he went on to Sault Ste. Marie, arriving there on July 4, only to learn that this old mission post was also to be, temporarily at least, without a priest. Fervently he prayed to God that others might heed the Divine call and come to this vineyard, which was so overburdened with fruit.

On July 27, he arrived at La Pointe, Madeline Island, Wisconsin. He was the first priest to visit here in about one hundred and sixty years, the first Catholic missionary since the days of Fathers Marquette and Allouez.[1] With few adherents, without church or abode, and with only three dollars in his pockets, he courageously began his labors. He found the Chippewa Indians not only well disposed toward religion but even willing, after a little encouragement, to help him to build a church.

Notwithstanding the fact that it had been made with crude materials, shaped by the few tools available, and had been erected by the unskilled labor of the Indians, the church was completed within a week. On August 9, it was dedicated in honor of Saint Joseph. Unrefined as the structure appeared, its purpose was symbolized by a fairly high steeple in which was mounted a bell that Father Baraga had transported from Detroit.

His pleasing personality, as well as his sincerity and his tactful use of their language, differing but slightly from the Ottawa, soon won the confidence of the natives. In a little over two months he had baptized one hundred and ninety-six of them, a glorious harvest of souls!

To his own comfort he gave little thought, but the sight of the half-naked children running about in the cold grieved him intensely. Because the climate in this part of the country was so unfavorable to agriculture, the poor Indians, far removed from the centers of civilization, could buy, with their meager products, very few of the necessities of life. Oh, how fervently he prayed that he might clothe these children and win thereby their parents' goodwill! Yet all this time, his own winter clothes, which were to have been forwarded to him, failed to arrive and he himself suffered from the cold.

He extended his activities to Fond-du-Lac, Minnesota, a trading post about ninety miles west from La Pointe, on the southwestern edge of the present city of Duluth. A trader, Pierre Cotte, whose piety distinguished him from the general run of men of his calling, had taught the Fond-du-Lac Indians to sing and to pray from an Indian prayer book, published by Father Baraga in 1832. His book fortunately had come into the trader's possession. In spite of well financed Protestant activity and of Father Baraga's necessarily infrequent visits, the efforts of this pious trader were instrumental in winning many to the Catholic faith.

During the evenings of the month before Christmas, Father Baraga visited a settlement, three miles distant, where he instructed the natives in the catechism. The six-mile walk was made in very cold weather, and, as the instructions were lengthy, he returned home late. For all these sacrifices he was well repaid however; for on Christmas Day he baptized twenty-two persons, the majority of whom were adults. He allowed himself, in fact, little rest, for in addition to his many pastoral and missionary duties, he engaged in literary work by preparing several books for publication.

His first year's labors brought the light of Christianity to two hundred and fifty souls. Soon the rapidly increasing number of converts created a serious problem. Although he was now "confronted with the pleasant necessity of enlarging the church," he found himself without the means of financing such a project. From the poor Indians, many of whom were objects of charity, he could expect little, if any, monetary aid. No other course remained open to him but to appeal again to his foreign friends and benefactors. Feeling justified by the conditions, he decided to go to Europe himself. On September 29, 1836, he left the Chippewas and traveled by boat to Detroit. From there to New York he traveled on a railroad train for the first time in his life.

Mary and Joseph Gregorich on their twenty-fifth
wedding anniversary, August 1945

Joseph Gregorich and Rev. Zaplotnick, another Baraga Historian,
comparing notes. (1952)

The Bishop Baraga House was built in 1855. It became the home of Bishop Baraga in 1866, when the headquarters of the Catholic Diocese of the Upper Peninsula was transferred to Marquette from Sault Ste. Marie. Bishop Frederic Baraga died in the front right room on January 19, 1868.

Church of the Holy Name, L'Anse, Michigan, built by Father Baraga. Drawing by Fr. Otto Skolla O.F.M. (1845)

Holy Redeemer Mission Church, in Eagle Harbor, was built in 1854 on land purchased by Frederic Baraga in 1852. It is thought that Father Baraga was at this site when he learned of his confirmation by the Pope of his nomination as Bishop of Upper Michigan on 6 October 1853. It is the oldest of the remaining churches actually built by Bishop Baraga still in use. Mass is celebrated each Saturday during the summer months.

The chalice and paten presented to Bishop Baraga by the Austrian Emperor Francis Joseph, on the occasion of the Emperor's wedding to princess Elizabeth of Bavaria, which Bishop Baraga attended.

The Eucharist being celebrated in front of Bishop Baraga's tomb in the Bishop's Crypt, St. Peter's Cathedral, Marquette Michigan.

Some members of the Bishop Baraga Association at an event commemorating the one hundredth anniversary of Baraga's death in 1968. Joseph Gregorich is seated in the center of the first row.

Joseph and Mary Gregorich with daughter Pauline on Mary and Joseph's fiftieth wedding anniversary, August 1970.

Coat of Arms of Bishop Baraga

For his motto Bishop Baraga chose Luke 10:42
UNIM EST NECESSARIUM: ONE THING IS NECESSARY.
The love of God and love for God's children was the center of
Baraga's life. His devotion to the Blessed Mother was part of his
dedication to her Divine Son.
On the left field of the coat of arms is the IHS for Christ; on the right
field is the AM for Mary whom he hailed in his Ave Marias daily.
The cross and three nails on the left field symbolize the instruments
of Christ's crucifixion. The sword which pierced Mary's heart at
that crucifixion and the star which symbolizes her triumphant
queenship appear in the right field. In the bottom half are the symbols
of FAITH, HOPE and CHARITY: the cross, the anchor and the heart.

Photograph of Bishop Baraga taken in the last years of his life showing the effects of a life of much physical hardship.

Prayer

Heavenly Father, your servant Bishop Frederic Baraga desired to live a life of total commitment to your Son Jesus Christ, Our Lord. He dedicated himself completely to missionary activity to make you known, loved and served by the original peoples in the land of the Great Lakes.

Bishop Baraga brought peace and love wherever he traveled, Teach me to spread peace and love in our human family. Fill me with the spirit of prayer which was so much a part of his life and which drew him into an intimate union with Jesus Christ, your Son. Help me to accept the hardships of life as willingly as he did and thereby die to self that I may rise with Christ in glory.

Grant that your servant, Frederic Baraga, may be raised to the honors of the altar and through his intercession grant the graces and favors for which I now pray.
Grant this through our Lord Jesus Christ. Amen

Once across the Atlantic Ocean, he remained for two months in Paris, while supervising the printing of his Chippewa and Ottawa prayer books. From Paris he went by way of Rome to his native Slovenia. In Ljubljana, its capital, and in other places as well, he preached and lectured on Indian missions to multitudes of the faithful. At Trebnje and Dobrnia he visited his relatives, prayed most devoutly in his old parish church, and renewed his vows at the baptismal font, where he had been baptized.

That his fame had preceded him to Vienna was evidenced by the reception accorded him. After giving an account of his labors to his sponsors, the Leopoldine Society, this humble priest was received by the royal family and honored by the renowned Prince Metternich.[2] The missionary was showered with gifts from all parts of the Austrian empire, and was given a large sum of money, amounting approximately to twenty-five hundred dollars.

Notes:
1. La Pointe is a town on Madeline Island, one of the Apostle Islands in Lake Superior off the Wisconsin shore.
2. Prince Klemens von Metternich (1773-1859) an Austrian nobleman, was one of the leading statesmen in Europe in the 19th century. He played a key role in securing peace and order in Europe after the defeat of Napoleon.

CHAPTER XIII

A Parish in the Wilderness

Greatly pleased with the result of his visit to Europe, Father Baraga turned toward his New World home. Sailing from Le Havre on May 24, 1837, he arrived in New York on July 10. The return trip into the wilderness proved tedious and long and was accompanied by much delay, because of the difficulty of transporting his bulky church goods. With him also came his sister, Antonia, and Andrew Cesirek who offered to act as his servant. The servant, after remaining with him for about a year, left him, presumably, because Father Baraga lived so meagerly and poorly. His sister assisted him in teaching school, but after she had found that the rigors of the climate strained her health, she settled in Philadelphia, where she opened a private school for girls.

On October 8, 1837, Father Baraga was settled again in La Pointe, after being away for a little more than a year. As winter was right at his heels, he did not begin work on the church until the following spring, when he personally supervised the construction, besides performing his priestly duties. By his own industry he inspired the Indians, who, since they were by nature an indolent lot, disliked to work steadily.

When the church was completed on the first Sunday in September, 1838, a solemn day of dedication and a feast of thanksgiving were observed. While the exterior was rough-looking, the inside, plastered and white-washed, had been decorated with oil paintings which Fr. Baraga had brought with him from Europe. Later the church was improved with a new altar, pews and a pulpit, the last being a genuine novelty for that part of the country in those days.

The week after the dedication, when Bishop Rese made an unexpected visit to La Pointe, the Indians welcomed him with reverence and joy. They had never seen a bishop, but Father Baraga had spoken often to them of the Apostles of the Church, particularly when he was instructing them on the Sacrament of Confirmation. Soon after the bishop had confirmed a class of one hundred and twelve, he left La Pointe, that he might take advantage of available transportation. Before leaving, he appointed Father Baraga his Vicar General for Northern Wisconsin, in recognition of the distinguished services the missionary had rendered.[1]

Within the next few years this mission post developed into a well organized parish. It had its trustees, sexton, mass servers and a trained choir of male voices under a paid director, as do the parishes of our day. Father Baraga also bought a bell, weighing four hundred and seventy pounds, whose tones awed the Indians when they first heard its echoing peals ring through the still air.

But before the remodeled church was three years old, the parish had again outgrown its place of worship. As it was poorly built by the unskilled labor in the past, Father Baraga now resolved to tear it down and, with additional material, to build a larger edifice at a more convenient location. This new church, upon completion, was dedicated the first Sunday in August, 1841. Its cost was greater than estimated, and the expected foreign donations were not forthcoming. His creditors pressed him for payment. This mercenary attitude tried his good, but sensitive nature. In a

letter to the Archbishop of Vienna, director of the Leopoldine
Society, he gave way to his feelings and wrote touchingly, that he
asked for nothing for himself but only for his poor people who,
because of their penurious circumstances were unable to pay for
the church themselves. His pathetic plea brought him the
necessary aid.

About this time he began the practice of devoting the first
hours of the day to prayer, a saintly habit which he observed until
his death. In the summer he arose usually at three o'clock, in the
winter at four, and would pray one or two hours and, at times,
even three. He prayed no matter where he might have been, in his
private chapel or under open skies, on the shore of a lake or in the
dense forest, in fair or in stormy weather, in a corner of a crowded
inn or alone in the wilderness. Whether he had retired early or late,
the early morning would find him kneeling in sweet communica-
tion with Our Lord. Small wonder was it, then, that this saintly
man with so great a love of prayer had the grace to soften the most
hardened of hearts and the power to instill the faith deep into the
very core of human nature.

La Pointe was later incorporated into the Diocese of
Milwaukee, and, although Father Baraga, at the time of the incor-
poration, was stationed at L'Anse,[2] he retained his former pastorate
for some time and visited it at intervals. Bishop Henni made an
episcopal visit there in 1844 and was pleased with the conditions
as he found them.[3] He stated that the church at La Pointe was
much nicer than his cathedral. This remark not only indicated the
poverty of his own diocese but was a tribute to Father Baraga's
industry and achievement. The church, built in 1841, was burned
to the ground in 1901 by the enemies of the faith, although it had

been well preserved to that time.

Father Baraga's eight years at La Pointe were fruitful ones. Coming here almost penniless, among a strange and non-Catholic people, he succeeded in establishing a parish, in building a school, a comfortable parsonage, and, considering the time and location, a monumental church. These achievements, well worthy of a life's labor, might have led him to settle down to the routine life of a parish priest. But Father Baraga's missionary spirit would not permit such a course. Leaving the comparative ease and comfort he enjoyed here, he again faced hardships and privations, that he might avail himself of the greater opportunities in the missionary field.

Notes:
1. Bishop Baraga was appointed Vicar General of the Diocese of Detroit. A Vicar General is the highest office in a diocese after the ordinary (bishop of the diocese). He is deputed to exercise the episcopal jurisdiction in the name of the bishop, so that his acts are reputed to be acts of the bishop himself.
2. L'Anse was an Indian settlement at the head of Keweenaw Bay in Lake Superior off the Michigan Shore.
3. Bishop John Martin Henni (1805-1881) was the first bishop in Wisconsin and the first Archbishop of Milwaukee.

CHAPTER XIV

The Beginning of the Famous L'Anse Mission

Father Baraga often received petitions, either by mail, messenger or report, from distant settlements that yearned for someone to bring them the Word of God. One such persistent request came from L'Anse, a trading post at the head of Keweenaw Bay, about one hundred and eighty miles east of La Pointe. A trading company had established an outpost there. Its agent, Philip Crebassa, who was a good Catholic, had the habit of frequently reading the Bible on Sunday to an Indian chieftan. At the request of the Indian, the trader petitioned Father Baraga to make a missionary visit to L'Anse.

At first, his priestly duties at La Pointe prevented him from accepting the invitation, but by July of 1843, when conversions were few due to the fact that nearly all the natives at this mission had become Christians, he decided to make the visit. This decision was hastened by his knowledge that a Protestant missionary had settled there. Father Baraga was but the second Catholic missionary to set foot on the soil at L'Anse. The first had been Father Rene Menard, who had come here about one hundred and eighty years earlier, and who either perished in the wilderness or was murdered by the Indians. Mr. Crebassa made preparations for Father Baraga's coming by adapting a part of his house for use as a chapel and school. During his brief initial visit of three weeks, the missionary christened thirty, besides leaving many others in a receptive mood.

He returned to La Pointe, but, after considering how well inclined toward Christianity the Indians at L'Anse were, his zeal bade him to leave La Pointe and go to this practically virgin missionary field. In contrast to his first visit, the Indians greeted him warmly, when, on October 24, in the same year, he returned to establish a permanent mission. He set himself to work, and with the help of some able companions who had accompanied him, he opened a school. More than fifty students, including twelve adults, made up the first class.

Once more he faced the task of building a church in a community where Christianity was just getting a foothold, and again he was compelled to beg for aid. Entreatingly he wrote: "The salvation of a single soul is worth infinitely more than all the money in the world." How could his benefactors refuse his petitions when he placed so high a value on a soul; when, with the expenditure of only a few hundred dollars, he was saving many from eternal perdition?

For definite reasons he decided to build across the bay, on the west side. With the financial aid of his European sponsors he was able to complete the church during the following summer, and dedicate it to the Holy Name of Jesus, on September 29, 1844.

It was clear to him that, if an Indian were to remain a good Christian, the native had to be removed from evil influences and from pagan surroundings. If an Indian were to continue living in a hut, which Father Baraga compared to a "bear-lair," and continued cultivating primitive habits in keeping with his surroundings, he could not be expected to live a God-fearing Christian life. Father Baraga planned, therefore, to build fifteen houses for his new converts and to give them a plot of ground to be planted and cultivated, in the hope that, in such an environment, they might improve their living conditions and live a peaceful Christian life.

At first such an undertaking seemed impractical, involving much work and expense. Father Baraga, however, was equal to the task. With the aid of liberal foreign donations, the first group of houses was completed by the time the church was dedicated. Later more dwellings of a similar type were added to the settlement.

The Indians soon changed their habits. Before their conversion the men did nothing but hunt or smoke while lolling in the wigwams. The women did almost all the work. But the religion of Christ taught the haughty braves that all must work and pray. The men, accordingly, became industrious. They tilled the soil and tended to the livestock. The women, on their part, kept their houses neat and cared for their children. Thus, simultaneously with their conversion to Christianity, they were started on the road to a civilized way of life.

L'Anse was for Father Baraga a sad, sterile and unpleasant place, to which nothing but his pity for the poor neglected souls had attracted him. Wanting in many comforts and often destitute of the bare necessities of life, he would console himself with the thought of what joy would be his when, on Judgment Day, he would face his rigorous Judge by the side of those whom he had brought to His fold. "Oh, how I thank God," he would reflect, "for calling me to this laborious but highly consoling missionary state."

CHAPTER XV

Lauded for His Successful Labors

Although general conditions were not so bad at L'Anse as they had been at Grand River, the many whites in the settlement across the bay made the work of Father Baraga more difficult, since some of them were the cause of much drunkenness among the Indians. To cope effectively with this situation, Father Baraga organized a temperance society. He was aided in this work by the bishop who, during one of his visits, solemnly initiated the members as he stood in his pontifical robes at the communion railing and blessed each candidate.

Three years later Father Baraga noted that many of the Indians had kept their pledge faithfully. Unscrupulous whites offered them valuable presents, if only they would drink. Sometimes these wicked persons even tried to compel them to drink by threatening them with blows. Nevertheless, the good Indians, although tempted and maltreated, refused to indulge in liquor. They had overcome successfully their natural weakness for this vice, for now they hated it as much as they had loved it formerly.

While at L'Anse, Father Baraga wrote his most noted Indian books, the *Chippewa Grammar* and the *Chippewa Dictionary*, of which more will be said later. From here, as he had done from La Pointe, he made a number of long missionary journeys. Besides the nearby missions, he visited Fond-du-Lac and

Grand Portage, Minnesota; Fort Williams, Ontario; and his former mission post, La Pointe. One winter he made a trip which he estimated to have covered a distance of six hundred and ninety miles.

Protestant missionaries caused him deep concern. Jealous of his success, they slandered him and put obstacles in his way. Thus, after Father Baraga had built a church at the Bad River Indian settlement, it was taken over forcibly by his enemies upon its completion and was turned into a stable.[1] The culprits were aided and abetted both by the Protestant missionary and by government officials.

His work at L'Anse merited for him universal praise. The public at large became interested in his labors. Christian and pagan, Catholic and non-Catholic, alike respected this missionary and held him in high esteem. An estimation of his work, printed in a Catholic publication of the day, reads as follows;

"Frederick Baraga, Vicar General of the Diocese of Detroit, and a most worthy missionary priest, opened a mission at L'Anse about a year ago amid incredible labor and hardships. He had built a church and schoolhouse and has the consolation of having charge of more than thirty-three Chippewa families that he himself has converted to the faith, and he has the assured hope that this flock will be increased by new conversions. The quick advancement in civilization and prosperity of these people whose missions have been lately founded, has been the subject of wonder to all who have known L'Anse these last two years, for the Indians have entirely abandoned their savage customs, ways and irregular mode of life, and have become a good, industrious, self-supporting, honest and sober class of people. They now live in decent homes and work their lands industriously."

Non-Catholic publications also lauded him and held him up as a model missionary. An extract from one such article, with corrections in parentheses, is given below:

"...it is more apparent in a Catholic missionary that he devotes himself wholly and entirely to the cause which he promotes, since he labors continually for others, since he fearlessly exposes his health to danger in the service of the sick and dying, and since he is more willing at all times to suffer privations. An example of this kind is told of Father Baraga at Keweenaw Point, a man almost sixty years of age, who devotes the whole of his large income, as also his personal services, to the cause he has taken upon himself, and receives no compensation for same. Last winter he went on snowshoes from L'Anse to Copper Harbor, a distance of fifty-seven miles, through an uninhabited region, solely to baptize a child, of whom he had heard that it would probably die. Such proofs of self-sacrifice are not without influence on the observant eye of the Indian..." Referring to the above quotation, Father Baraga was only 51 years old at the time, but his strenuous life aged him rapidly. Also the indication of a large income refers to donations from the Leopoldine Society.

The active development of the rich copper deposits on Keweenaw Point, which began about 1845, ushered in a new era for the Lake Superior country. People flocked to the mines in a general land boom that was promoted.

Advised of this activity, Father Baraga visited the Point in January of 1847, and was surprised at the rapid development of this rich mining district. He went from mine to mine, preaching and ministering to the spiritual needs of the people. As a large part of those employed at the mines were Irish, French or German, he had to put his linguistic ability to good use, sometimes preaching in three languages in one day. From this and subsequent visits of his arose the many churches now found on the Point.

Note:
  1. Bad River Indian Settlement was located near the present day Ashland, Wisconsin.

CHAPTER XVI

His Arduous and Perilous Missionary Journeys

The accounts of Father Baraga's missionary travels, particularly those during the long and severely cold winters of that region, are tales of pitiful hardships, intense sufferings and almost superhuman endurance. Some of these frequent journeys of his were hundreds of miles long. Often he traveled on heavy cumbersome snowshoes, as much as forty miles in a single day.

With his vestments, provisions and blanket in a pack strapped to his back, he would trudge along the shores of the lake, or over the ice, or through dense forests, sometimes for three or four days before reaching a human habitation or settlement. Many a night he slept out in the open, underneath the starry sky, on the hard, frozen ground or snow, suffering from the cold, since he could not carry blankets enough to keep himself comfortable. At times, upon awakening, he would find himself even covered with snow. On several occasions he nearly lost his life in a blizzard, so common in that part of the country. In the clouds of blinding snow he lost his way time and time again, but a kind Providence always led him back to the trail. More than one such blizzard found him far from a human habitation, almost exhausted and suffering from the intense cold that reached as low as twenty to forty degrees below zero. To stop meant to freeze. In such cases there was no other choice left him but to plod on as long as a spark of life remained.

An example of his many agonizing experiences was his walk of thirty miles to the next house on one of his missionary tours. Although he had started early in the morning, at dusk he was still fifteen miles away from his destination and about an equal distance from any other human habitation. His way lay over a wind-swept, ice-covered lake, where the strong, biting head wind "threatened to freeze the very blood in my veins."

What was he to do? Tired as he was from the day's fatiguing walk, he dared not stop, for he would freeze. With supreme confidence in his deliverance, Father Baraga trudged on, while his ebbing energy increased his exertion and lessened his progress. The last seven miles he walked at the rate of a mile an hour. His trust in God had not been in vain, however, for he arrived safely at his destination, although utterly exhausted. Luckily, he suffered no ill effects from his distressing experience except that, later, his face peeled.

A trader and government employee, who had lived for the greatest part of the last century in the vicinity of La Pointe, in his reminiscences praises the Catholic missionaries, and Father Baraga in particular. "...I am not in the least prejudiced in saying so, for the information of truthfulness in their dealing I get from the Indians themselves...One incident I will relate which came directly my way, in the winter of 1853, that shows one man at least whose heart was true to his teachings. It was a very hard and cold winter, and many Indians were poor and destitute, particularly so at Fond-du-Lac, at the head of Lake Superior. By some means, Father Baraga, a Catholic priest located at L'Anse Bay, a distance by trail from Fond-du-Lac of about two hundred and fifty miles, heard of the great sufferings there and that one family in particular, a widow with her children, were all sick. He provided himself with such medicines as could readily be had and set out on snowshoes to make the journey in the dead of winter, with the snow several feet deep. About the 20th of January, 1854, I left La Pointe for Ontonagon, some ninety miles away in the direction of L'Anse. About halfway between La Pointe and Ontonagon, I met Father Baraga on his way to Fond-du-Lac, as he said, to assist the distressed and the needy there. I am quite positive that he would have perished that night but for our meeting. His snowshoes had given out, and it would have been impossible for him to have proceeded far without them on account of the deep snow...I have been frequently told by the Indians that such acts of kindness as Father Baraga displayed, but not to such a hazardous degree, were common with the Catholic missionaries."

His missionary travels abound in many such trying incidents. Although many heroic tales have been told of this saintly missionary, countless others shall remain untold as, in his humble reticence, he seldom spoke or wrote of them himself.

In spite of the perils and hardships, he never shirked a duty. Without a murmur he went on, thanking God for the privilege of laboring and suffering for His Name. Yet, he did have one complaint to make, — he found it very difficult to read his breviary by the poor, flickering light of the camp-fire. After a day of wearisome travel, after his body was aching and though he was almost exhausted, he would not retire without reading the *Divine Office*[1] . Again, about four o'clock in the morning, he could be found kneeling on the cold, frozen ground, deeply engrossed in prayer. It was in prayer that he found not only consolation for all that he suffered but also strength for his weakened body. To talk thus to his Master rekindled his ever-burning missionary zeal into a flame.

Note:
1. The former name for the official daily liturgical prayer by which the Church sanctifies the hours of the day. Since Vatican II this prayer is entitled *The Liturgy of the Hours.*

CHAPTER XVII

Remarkable Deliverances

During his adventurous missionary life, Father Baraga narrowly escaped death a number of times in a manner that might be considered almost miraculous. Because of his aversion to idleness, he disregarded the weather. To save time, he risked his life. At such times his trust in God never faltered, even if he was facing almost certain death.

One of his perilous experiences was to be marooned on the lake upon a floating cake of ice. On this occasion, accompanied by a Chippewa Indian guide, he was traveling from La Pointe to Ontonagon. It was at the winter's end. The lake was, indeed, still frozen, but the ice was spongy and dangerous. Disregarding the peril, however, Father Baraga chose to cross the lake on the ice in preference to taking the circuitous and more tiresome road along the sandy beach.

After traveling for some time, he and the guide noticed that the ice had broken away from the mainland, for they could see the blue waters of the lake between them and the shore. As the wind was blowing off-shore and toward mid-lake, where the ice would be broken up, the guide became alarmed, and felt quite certain that they were doomed. Calmly, Father Baraga quieted his excited companion, and after assuring him that God would protect them, he sang Chippewa hymns to allay the guide's fears.

Soon the wind veered and blew in the direction toward which they were heading. Thus they reached their destination safely the very same day. "You see," said Father Baraga gleefully, "we have traveled far and yet worked but little."

Another noteworthy experience occurred on his journey from La Pointe to Grand Portage, Minnesota, in the year 1846. Contrary to the warning and the advice of the Indians he made preparations to cross the lake in a small, flat-bottomed rowboat, fitted with a mast and sail, a craft hardly fit for so venturesome a journey. A short cut across the lake would mean a saving of from three to five days of travel. To Father Baraga, who devoted all his time and energy to the cause of his Master, this economy of time was well worth the risk.

On a calm day, accompanied by a tried and faithful guide, he left Sand Island, one of the Apostle Islands, northwest of La Pointe. After a time a strong wind began to blow and Lake Superior became rough. When they had reached mid-lake, the wind had gathered the fury of a storm, and the guide, becoming frightened, exclaimed: "Father, perhaps we are going to perish!" The missionary, who though uncomfortably situated, was deeply engrossed in prayer, looked up and replied reassuringly: "Do not be afraid. The 'black-robe' will not die in the water, for if he did, the people on the other side would be unfortunate."

The storm raged for the remainder of the trip, driving them far off their course. At the sight of land, the experienced eye of the guide sensed another danger, one even greater than what they had survived, for he saw the turbulent waters becoming roaring breakers as they crashed upon the cragged shore. In a quandary, he asked the Father where he was to steer the craft. The missionary, still praying fervently and without looking up, answered as if he had been inspired, "Straight ahead."

The unseen hand of God grasped the rudder and steered them safely past the breakers. That hand guided them, in their frail craft, straight into the mouth of a then unnamed river. In gratitude for their deliverance, they erected, on the point of the landing, a cross made of boughs. This rude, inartistic emblem of their faith gave this stream its name of Cross River, which it retains to this day. The village of Schroeder, Minnesota, on the beautiful modern highway that runs along the northern shore of the lake, is located near the mouth of Cross River.

CHAPTER XVIII

The Father of Indian Literature

In so wild and forlorn country as this, among the poor and uneducated Indians, where human beings were living in a most primitive manner, apart from civilization and the rest of the world, culture and refinement might be expected to deteriorate while such an environment was tending to deepen its impression as time went on. But Father Baraga was immune to any such degradation of spirit. His untiring labors prevented his stagnation. His requited love for the Indians inspired him not only to religious but also to literary and scientific achievement.

His active missionary life allowed him little leisure. Nevertheless, his literary fame was earned in his spare moments, particularly in the long winter evenings. He was occupied constantly with some useful work. This ceaseless activity, unselfishly devoted to the betterment of mankind and to the glory of God, has been appropriately described by one of his biographers as "sanctity in action."

Although his fame as a writer and a linguist is eclipsed somewhat by his success as a missionary, still his literary work alone would suffice to preserve his name to posterity. From early life he had proved himself a talented man of letters and had become proficient in Slovene, German, Latin, French, English and Italian, a linguistic foundation which enabled him to become an authority on the Chippewa Indian language.

In gratitude to his Austrian sponsors he wrote, in German, a work entitled, *The History, Character, Life and Manners of the North American Indians,* which together with the Slovene translation thereof, was printed in Ljubljana in 1837. A French translation was printed in Paris in the same year. For his people, relatives, friends and former parishioners in Slovenia, he wrote three other prayer books filled with holy and pious thoughts. "Accept these books," he wrote, "that I have written for you in this far-off land, as an indication of my great love for you and my earnest desire for your eternal salvation, my beloved, never-to-be-forgotten Slovenes."

Being a writer, it was but natural that he interested himself in Indian literature. Soon after beginning his missionary labors, he realized that suitable books were necessary for his missions. After only a year among the Ottawas, and his knowledge of the language at that time was limited, he wrote his first Indian prayer book. Four years later he enlarged, revised and rewrote the book in Chippewa and Ottawa. Several editions were printed during Father Baraga's lifetime. This prayer book was treasured and cherished by the Indians, who frequently requested that it be placed on their breasts when they were laid in their final resting place.

As the education of the Indians progressed, the need of more books became apparent, and he applied himself diligently to satisfy the necessity. He wrote the *Gagikwe Masinaigan,* or Sermon Book, containing abstracts from the Old and New Testaments and the Epistles and Gospels for the year. This book was used extensively in Indian schools. The last edition, published in 1858, was in use throughout the 19th century. The *Life of Jesus Christ* a book of sermons for the Cree Indians and *Eternal Truths,* a small catechism for school use, were some of his other literary contributions to the advancement of the Indian.

The rapid growth of Christianity among the natives emphasized more strongly the scarcity of priests. This exigency was made more acute because it took the newcomers so much time to master the difficult Indian language before they could perform their missionary duties with efficiency. Considering that some of the words have thousands of terminations and that some are very long, as for example, "mitchikanakobidjigan" meaning "fence," one can imagine the difficulty of the language. A further obstacle at the time arose from the lack of suitable textbooks on the subject.

At the insistance of the bishop and inspired by noble impulses, Father Baraga's keen, analytical and systematic mind produced what may be called, with truth, the foundation of Indian literature, a *Grammar of the Ojibway (Chippewa) Language.* Beginning at the very bottom, with his main source of information no more than answers to his countless queries by those who had no idea what a grammar was, he successfully completed this ardu- ous task. This work, so capably and thoroughly accomplished, is prized highly by philologists to this day as a distinctive contribution to linguistics. It has earned for its author the title of "The Father of Indian Literature."

He added luster to his fame a few years later, by the publication of his *Dictionary of the Ojibway Language.*[1] This comprehensive work was compiled with much painstaking labor and perseverance, extending over a number of years. Because of its thoroughness it is to this day regarded as a standard work.

These Indian books played an important part in Christianizing and civilizing the Indians. It has been estimated roughly that approximately twenty thousand natives benefited by these products of Father Baraga's zeal, industry, talents and self-sacrificing labors.

His letters to the Leopoldine Society of Vienna played a leading role in the promotion and support of the American Indian missions. In them he expressed his lofty hopes, masterfully delivered his pleas, and vividly described his labors. Published in a number of languages and widely distributed, they were the means of attracting a large number of missionaries to the New World. From his native land of Slovenia alone, more than twenty came, among them being Pierz, Mrak, Vertin, Skolla, Lautizar, Chebul, Buh, Trobec, Tomazin and Zuzek.

Not only in this country, but in Europe also, the name of Father Baraga was widely known. The people were eager to read of him, a man whom they regarded and revered as a model missionary.

Note:
1. *The Dictionary of the Ojibway Language* is still in print.

CHAPTER XIX

A Bishop to the Indians

On July 29, 1853, the Upper Michigan Peninsula was made a Vicariate Apostolic, and, as might have been expected, Father Baraga, who had labored in that vicinity for more than twenty years, was named its first bishop.[1] On the feast of All

Saints, in the same year, he was consecrated in the metropolitan Church, in Cincinnati, Ohio, as titular bishop of Amyzonia.

The neighboring bishops ceded parts of their dioceses to this new vicariate, placing under Bishop Baraga's care a portion of the lower Michigan Peninsula and practically all the country around Lake Superior, where the greater part of the Indians had settled. In reality, he became a bishop to the Indians.

The care for the spiritual welfare of the souls in this vast, sparsely settled territory was thus heaped upon his willing shoulders. In this embryo vicariate he needed money for the purchase of land for schools and churches, for the construction of the buildings, as well as for vestments and other church necessities. His people could not be expected to provide these funds. They were too poor. The Indians barely eked out an existence, whereas the white Catholics, who, for the most part, were poorly paid day laborers in the mines, were in need of many things themselves.

In addition to his need for funds, the many converts and the steady influx of the whites, with only two priests to minister to them, accented the urgent necessity for more missionaries. Knowing the conditions as Bishop Baraga did, he realized that he must obtain aid. But, from where? In all this wide world he had no one to whom he could turn except his friends and benefactors in Europe, who had aided him so generously in the past. He resolved that he would beg them, on bended knees if need be, to have pity for his poor Indians. The stringency of the situation urged him to leave Cincinnati immediately for Europe.

Before starting for New York, he wrote two pastoral letters, the one to the whites, the other to the Indians. To read the latter, a pastoral letter which, perhaps, is without a parallel, reveals a masterly use of the Chippewa language. The simple, plain words effectively grouped, conveyed his fatherly message concerning the virtues of faith, prayer, respect for the Holy Name, obedience and the love of God, in terms adapted to the level of understanding of his readers. He affectionately called them his children and publicly proclaimed his love for them. This love was the motivating force that spurred him onward to work for their salvation.

Arriving in Liverpool for his second European visit, he went first to Dublin, after which he toured the continent and stopped in the large cities to present his pleas and to seek to interest priests in his missions. When he reached Vienna, he gave again an account of his labors to the Leopoldine Society. He described the deplorable conditions in his new vicariate. He pictured vividly the bright prospect of the future while stressing the present need of liberal support. His earnest and sincere pleas brought forth a generous response. He was literally showered with gifts.

Arriving in Slovenia, on January 27, 1854, he celebrated Mass as a bishop at the same altar where he had celebeated his first Mass, thirty years before. In the parish church at Dobrnic, he knelt once more in prayer and meditation at the baptismal font, "in gratitude for the infinite grace of my regeneration." At Saint Martin's and at Metlika he preached in churches crowded with people who had come from near and far to hear their former curate. Although all wished to hear him talk of his own missionary work, he, because of his modesty, seldom mentioned it. The honors that were bestowed upon him and the ovations that greeted him wherever he went would have made others vain in their glory.

In Rome he was received twice in audience by the Holy

Father, Pope Pius IX, who, from the hands of the Indian bishop, graciously accepted as a gift the first copies of the *Chippewa Grammar* and the *Chippewa Dictionary*. The Holy Father honored his faithful, humble servant by presenting him with a beautiful chalice. Elated and happy, Bishop Baraga vowed that he would never part with this precious gift.

On his way back to America he again visited Vienna, where he was one of the seventy prelates to be present at the wedding of the emperor, Francis Joseph, to the Bavarian princess, Elizabeth. The royal pair entertained him and presented him with an episcopal ring, a pectoral cross and two chalices. The ring, set with an amethyst engraved with the name of Jesus and encircled with diamonds, is worn by his successors on festive occasions. The poverty of his Indians and his own humility prompted Bishop Baraga to part with the costly pectoral cross, richly studded with jewels. He procured, in its stead, a cheap imitation to serve as a remembrance of the sovereigns' generosity. One of the chalices is in the cathedral at Marquette.[2] The other was destroyed in a fire.

In Prague, the former emperor, Ferdinand, showed his regard for Bishop Baraga's missionary labors by giving him one thousand florins. The King of Bavaria invited him for a visit, and, after a hearty reception, presented him with some rich gifts. The Ludwig Mission Society swelled his fund by a contribution of two thousand florins.

And thus, this humble missionary, respected and loved by the Indians, was feted by nobles and honored by a king and by emperors. He, who had lived among uncultured and unrefined Indians, had been found worthy to be invited and welcomed into castles and palaces.

Satisfied with the results of his visit, he was now anxious to return to his beloved and needy Indians.

Notes:
1. Apostolic Vicariate is a territorial division of the Church that does not have the full status of a diocese. This occurs when a mission territory has been established in a country or other area that does not have an established hierarchy and shows potential for stability and growth.
2. The cherished chalice, as well as a pectoral cross and other Baraga Artifacts, can be viewed in Bishop Baraga Association offices in Marquette, Michigan.

CHAPTER XX

The Itinerant Bishop

After assembling in Paris his priests and others, whom he had adopted for his vicariate, he sailed for home. Toward the end of August, 1854, he arrived at Sault Ste. Marie, now the seat of his vicariate, eager to begin his work as a bishop. The townspeople greeted him with an ovation and staged a reception in his honor.

On his way to Sault Ste. Marie, he had visited Mackinac and Arbre Croche and in a few days was ready to continue his episcopal visits. He first went to La Pointe, where a joyous welcome awaited him. Happiness was added to the joy of the natives when they learned that their new bishop had brought them a resident priest, for these good Catholic Indians had been without one during the last year. As the new missionary could not speak the Chippewa tongue, Bishop Baraga was busy teaching, hearing confessions and preaching during his stay. Almost all availed themselves of the opportunity to receive the sacraments. Bishop Baraga also confirmed a class of one hundred, prepared by himself.

From La Pointe he went to Ontonagon, a flourishing town, where the people themselves had built a church in the hope that, by such a display of zeal, they would get a resident priest. The bishop was happy to be able to satisfy their desire. He left Father Dunne with them.

On his next trip he visited L'Anse, where great joy reigned when the natives beheld their former pastor, now their bishop. He reciprocated their feelings, and during the Confirmation service, with the miter on his head and the crozier in his hand, he spoke to them so tenderly that the stoic faces of the Indians gave way to their emotions. Even his own eyes were filled with tears.

From place to place he went, installing priests, establishing new congregations, building schools, churches and parsonages. When the need arose, he performed the duties of a missionary priest. He often preached, in one day's time, three or four sermons in as many different languages.

He was an itinerant bishop, seldom at home if it were possible to travel. In the summer of 1855, he traveled about eighteen hundred miles within three months time, covering much of the distance in a small open boat or canoe. He went as far south as Grand Traverse, Michigan, as far north as Fort Williams, Ontario, and east and west the length of Lake Superior.

His stays in Sault Ste. Marie during the summer were usually short, just long enough to care for matters requiring his attention. In the winter, when navigation on the lakes was closed, he took charge of the parish and performed pastoral duties, besides occupying himself with literary work. On occasion he would visit such nearby points as Saint Ignace and Mackinac. On one such trip, which he made in extremely cold weather, in a temperature of forty degrees below zero, he was forced to sleep out in the open, and his face nearly froze during the night.

White settlers began to pour into the region, particularly in the mining district. Bishop Baraga was expected to build churches and schools and to provide priests for them, but the growth of the vicariate was so rapid that, in a year, most of his money had been spent, and he faced again a shortage of priests.

His extremely sensitive nature was subject to many a shock during his career as bishop. Because of his own goodness and trusting nature, he was often taken advantage of and imposed upon. In addition, troubles with some of the priests and laity saddened him, so that he frequently entertained the thought of resigning. The troubles and disappointments in this rapidly growing vicariate proved a severe trial. Unceasingly he plodded on in the face of extreme difficulties and adversities, consoling himself with these lines, found in his diary under the date of March 7, 1857:

"With peaceful mind thy race of duty run;
God nothing does or suffers to be done,
That wouldst thyself, if thou couldst see
Through all events of things as well as He."

CHAPTER XXI

Work Was His Life

The marvelous growth of the vicariate so pleased the Holy Father, Pope Pius IX, that he, mindful of the future, raised it to the dignity of a diocese. On January 9, 1857, Bishop Baraga was named the first resident bishop of Sault Ste. Marie.

The period of greatest growth in the diocese was between the years 1856 and 1860. New settlements sprang up on the horizon. Towns grew like mushrooms. New parishes and missions were established. New churches were built and a number of old ones enlarged. The parishes in the mining districts prospered and were becoming more and more self-supporting. Some had fine, well built churches. One even boasted of a pipe organ, the first in the diocese.

When a new church was being contemplated, the name of Bishop Baraga usually headed the list of contributors with a liberal donation. In addition, he contributed to the support of most of the missions. Because of his generosity, he was frequently pressed for money, but his life of cares and sorrows was lightened by occasional gifts from the foreign mission societies, that made his own generosity possible.

A marked difference became evident in the lives of the Christian and non-Christian Indians. The Christians adopted the ways of civilization. They prospered and lived contentedly. The non-Christians eked out a miserable existence and were fast dying out. Pagan villages were being abandoned, whereas the settlements of the Christian Indians were spreading and growing. Unhappily, the intermingling with whites, particularly in the mining districts and among the Ottawas, where many saloons were to be found, exerted a baneful influence on the Indians.

The increase in intemperance threatened to destroy all the good that had been done. New Year's Day became a day of revelry and drunkenness. The Indians went from house to house, visiting, drinking and carousing. Bishop Baraga warned, preached and organized temperance societies, all to little effect. He foresaw what trouble and misery this vice would cause and his predictions were fulfilled direfully, until years later, the government was forced to take a hand in the matter. Long before the prohibition laws of the 1930's were passed, saloons in or near the Indian reservations were prohibited, and it was unlawful to sell liquor to an Indian anywhere.

But in spite of the ravages of this vice, the Indians acquired some of the industry of the white man and much of his skill at mechanical trades. The birchbark canoes were replaced by skillfully built boat. The churches erected by the Indians would have done credit to their white brothers.

The shortage of priests caused the bishop deep concern and grief. Since few priests volunteered for these missions, he had to depend to a great extent, on those he ordained himself. In his anxiety for the welfare of the diocese, he ordained, undoubtedly, some who were not fully prepared and adopted others without due investigation. Though his intentions were of the best, they sometimes turned into heartaches. As a missionary priest he had had only his own troubles, whereas now, on his weak, aging shoulders, lay heavily the cares of the whole diocese. With aching heart he lamented, "The past saddens me; the present torments me; and the future haunts me. I would infinitely prefer to be a missionary priest."

Although weighed down with age and cares, he worked with unabated zeal. One Sunday, June 10, 1860, he worked from four o'clock in the morning until ten at night. He heard many confessions, preached five sermons, baptized twenty-three and confirmed three. An extraordinary day! Work was his life, for he had once said, "Without work I cannot live."

CHAPTER XXII

Age and Hardships Begin to Levy Their Toll

His strenuous life, so full of hardships, had left its marks upon him. His health began to fail and his body began to waste. Some of the luster had gone from his eyes. Time had dug deep furrows in his face. In 1860 he was sixty-three years old, twenty-nine of which he had spent among the Indians.

His winter travels became increasingly difficult. Yet, he never hesitated to undertake a long journey to wherever he might do some good. In traveling over deep snow, his guides would go ahead of him and pack the snow and then wait for the feeble old bishop to catch up with them. Laboriously he would drag along the heavy, clumsy snowshoes, perspiring freely from the fatiguing walk.

When they halted, his clothes, wet with perspiration, would cause him to shiver as a leaf in a storm. The sight of this tired, venerable old man, scarcely able to stand, would have moved the most hardened to pity and compassion!

"How old age has affected me!" he wrote. "Formerly I could travel for weeks without feeling exhausted. Now a journey of two or three days tires me out."

After partaking of a frugal meal, usually consisting of tea and hard, dry bread, he would not fail to say his prayers and read the *Divine Office* while his guides prepared his bed of spruce boughs. He considered himself fortunate if he found an abandoned wigwam or hut in which to sleep, although even such nights proved far from providing comfort for him.

His episcopal dignity and his old age did not prevent him from practicing humility and mortification. Father Chebul told of some of his practices, two of which are mentioned here. When this young Father was ready to leave Sault Ste. Marie for his new mission post, the aged bishop carried Father Chebul's valises, even though the former protested strongly. With the heavy load he slipped and fell on the muddy road, and after being assisted to his feet and brushing off some of the mud, he insisted, to the embarrassment of the young Father, on carrying the valises the remainder of the way. Father Chebul tells also of the aged bishop's visit to where he later was stationed. On this occasion the bishop ordered the Father to sleep in the only bed available in the parsonage, while he himself slept on the floor with only a mat under him and a cloak for his cover. The bishop refused even a pillow. "You must spare yourself," he would say, "I am old and accustomed to such things. I am your bishop. You must obey."

This same priest recalled how God Himself had meted out swift punishment to one of the bishop's enemies. The bishop was endeavoring to straighten out a difficulty which had arisen between a priest in one of the parishes and himself, when a man, who was present and who sided with the priest, lost control of his temper and raised his hand as if to strike the aged bishop. The next day the man lost that arm in an accident at the mines.

With much satisfaction Bishop Baraga remembered the eighteenth anniversary of the beginning of his morning prayers and meditations which he had started while stationed at La Pointe. On one occasion he overslept, arising at five instead of three o'clock, for which oversight he rebuked himself with this note in his diary: "Two little hours, absolutely lost!"

CHAPTER XXIII

The Beginning of the End

In the early spring of 1861, Bishop Baraga left Sault Ste. Marie for Cincinnati. Traveling on foot to Alpena, about one hundred and fifty miles away, he was forced to wade through deep, soggy, melting snow that had made the roads almost impassable. The strain proved too much for him. He arrived in Alpena sick and exhausted and was forced to remain in bed for several days.

Sickness often overtook him on his journeys thereafter and sometimes while en route he would suffer from a pain in his chest, a sign that his end was near.

In Cincinnati he attended the Third Provincial Council. He preached the sermon at the Requiem Mass for the deceased prelates and also was commissioned to write to the Ludwig Mission Society in Bavaria, in the name of the Council. He remained in Cincinnati for two months, supervising the printing of some of his books. He also preached at a number of churches and gathered collections for his needy missions.

Although far from the battlefront, his diocese was affected by the Civil War which was then raging. The rising prices of commodities decreased the purchasing power of the dollar. Many of the able-bodied men had left to join the colors. Some of them returned home maimed. Families were placed in straitened circumstances and not a few became dependent upon charity. Still, though donations were fewer and smaller than before, his needs were greater.

The diocese was growing almost as fast as he could provide more priests. Cities and towns replaced former Indian settlements. The mining districts hummed with activity. Civilization was conquering the wilderness.

Some parishes became large enough to require the services of two priests, but because of the scarcity of ministers, one priest was obliged to do all the work of his own parish, besides caring for other missions which had no resident pastor. Thus, his Vicar General, Father Mrak, who later was to become his successor, had ten missions in addition to his own parish at Eagletown (Grand Traverse).

It was difficult for Bishop Baraga to find missionaries suitable for his remote diocese. A knowledge of English, French and German was desirable. In fact it was necessary, if the priest were to satisfy all the parishioners. Those stationed at the Indian missions had to master, in addition to the European languages, the difficult Chippewa tongue. There were few, indeed, who could satisfy all these requirements as effectively as did Bishop Baraga.

The severe winters and the attendant hardships of the missionary journeys, moreover, demanded a hardy, vigorous constitution that but a few priests possessed. And, as life here offered no worldly attractions, only those having a genuine missionary spirit came and stayed.

Support for the schools and the lack of efficient school teachers were also among the bishop's vexing problems. After unraveling much red tape, he succeeded in obtaining some government support for his Indian schools. The Protestant schools always had been favored in this respect. Sometimes he was compelled to use his newly ordained priests as teachers, while he acted as pastor and curate of his cathedral, besides attending to his many diocesan duties. When the Sisters of Saint Joseph offered to teach in two of his schools, he actually cried for joy.

This venerable, saintly bishop, though weakened by age, never ceased to practice self-denial, particularly that of fasting. Often he would go without food for two or three days, in addition to which he had abstained from meat for years!

CHAPTER XXIV

To the Last, A Missionary to the Indians

As the years passed, it became more and more evident that the seat of his diocese had been inconveniently located. At first Bishop Baraga had been reluctant to consider a change, but later, because of the poor transportation and the lack of mail facilities, and prompted by the appeals of his priests to move closer to them, he decided to petition Rome for permission to move to Marquette. This town, bearing the name of a famous Catholic missionary, had a large, new church, recently built and suitable for a cathedral. In addition, it was located more centrally, and was the terminal of a new railroad just being completed.

The petition was granted readily on October 23, 1866, but on condition that the name of Sault Ste. Marie be retained as a part of the designation of the new diocese. For this reason the diocese was called that of Sault Ste. Marie and Marquette until 1939.

On his coming to Marquette the following May, the citizens of the town, both Catholic and non-Catholic, planned to receive him with honor. Bishop Baraga's humility would not permit him, however, to accept such attention. He sternly forbade his people to make any preparations for a public reception.

His infirm and weak condition made impossible the long journeys on foot, such as he had made in the past, although his extensive diocese, with its many missions and parishes, demanded much of his attention. The railroads had penetrated this sparsely settled country and newly built roads had introduced new forms of transportation; the stagecoach and horseback riding, making traveling easier and more comfortable for the aged prelate.

At times he would lay aside his episcopal cares and resume his missionary labors among the Indians. He would visit the settlements on the islands near Sault Ste. Marie and on the Canadian and Michigan shores nearby, establish missions and build churches. Often repulsed and grieved because he encountered so many hardened Indians, who undoubtedly had been made averse to Christianity by having come into contact with bad Christians, both white and red, he nevertheless labored with an undaunted spirit and enjoyed a fair measure of success.

Much of the carpenter work on these new mission churches he did himself, such as making the tabernacle, the baptismal font, the frames for the altar cards and the Stations of the Cross, and the altar steps. He loved to work for the Indians. No work was too difficult, too tedious or too humble for this saintly bishop, if only, in the doing of it, he could aid in their salvation. Often he would say, even to the very last, "I am essentially an Indian missionary."

CHAPTER XXV

His Edifying Death

In the fall of 1866, the Second Plenary Council was convoked at Baltimore. Since he was in duty bound to be present, even though his advanced age and physical condition would hardly permit him to travel so long a distance, Bishop Baraga ventured to make the journey. Going by train by way of Chicago and accompanied by Father Bourion, who acted as his theologian, he arrived for the opening and solemn session on Sunday, October 7.

The third day, at the archiepiscopal residence, he suffered a severe stroke. He was found unconscious in a corridor at the foot of a stairway and was taken to Saint Agnes Hospital, where his condition was pronounced as critical. Archbishop Spaulding, who was presiding over the Council, requested prayers for the afflicted prelate.

Lying helpless and in pain, he was urged by the other bishops to spend the remainder of his life in a milder climate, since the cold wintry winds of Lake Superior would only hasten his end. He could not bear, however, the thought of being removed from his beloved people, especially from the Indians. As soon, therefore, as he regained some of his strength, he left almost fleeing from Baltimore, without making the customary call at the residence of the archbishop.

Throughout the return journey, he lay in the arms of Father Bourion, who, when changing trains, was forced to carry him from car to car. It did not seem possible that he could reach the end of his journey alive. But God had willed that he drain his cup of sorrows to the very bottom. Barely alive, he reached Marquette, only to find things in a turmoil and to learn that one of his priests had caused scandal and had left his post. This sad news brought bitter tears to his eyes and lessened his slim chance for recovery.

He lingered through the following year, at times gaining sufficient strength to walk a few paces up and down in his room. He spoke only with much difficulty. On November 11, of that year he insisted upon being carried to a train which would take him to Negaunee, about twelve miles away, to bless the cornerstone of a new church. Seated, he raised his trembling arms and, with a weak but clear voice, he asked for God's blessing as the multitude in reverential silence listened to his prayer.

Shortly before his death, he was visited by Father Terhorst, who was stationed at the time at the L'Anse Indian Mission. Bishop Baraga gave this priest all the money, about twenty dollars, that he still had, and requested that Father Terhorst use it for his Indian school. "But," objected Father Terhorst, "it is all the money you have. It would not be right for me to take it." "I do not need any more money," answered the bishop, "take it." This act, one of his last, indicated plainly his great unfading love for the Indians.

It was on the feast of the Holy Name of Jesus, January 19, 1868, that God called His faithful servant, then in his seventy-first year, to his rich eternal reward. He died as he had wished to die, penniless and obscure. Only Father Jacker, and Casper, the bishop's servant during his last years, were present at the end.

Although the coldness of the weather made it possible to

postpone the funeral for twelve days, only six priests were able to be present at the final services. The church was much too small for the event. The ceremonies were very simple, since the season of the year and the circumstances had prevented services befitting his rank. No bishop could reach Marquette in time for his burial.

Catholics and non-Catholics alike came to pay their respects to the man whose kindness and humility had won an affectionate place in all their hearts. It was a day of general mourning in Marquette. Many shops were closed and business was suspended by common agreement out of respect to his memory and in appreciation of his virtues and achievements.

His remains lie interred in the Bishops' Crypt in St. Peter Cathedral at Marquette.

CHAPTER XXVI

A Saintly Genius

So ended a life filled with noble achievements, a life unselfishly dedicated to the spreading of the Kingdom of God among men, a life rich in prayer and in acts of charity. So ended a saintly life, a life of self-denial, humility and obedience, a life fortified by an unbounded faith in its Master and filled to overflowing with a love for those less fortunate than itself.

Bishop Baraga, although educated, cultured and refined, chose to live a life most primitive, in a hut in the wilderness, among an unschooled people. He disowned riches to live in poverty. He preferred a life of hardships and privations to one of ease and plenty, and all this for the greater glory of God.

Beyond doubt, he was one of the greatest of Indian missionaries. His conversions, numbering thousands, and his literary works are the labors of a saintly genius. His efforts both directly and indirectly exerted an inestimable influence for good upon the lives of about twenty thousand Indians in the regions adjacent to the Upper Great Lakes. He loved them. They reciprocated his love and almost idolized the missionary, who had dedicated so nobly his life's labors to their spiritual and temporal well-being.

He was a pioneer. He built mission churches. Towns and cities grew around them. He was a harbinger of civilization, for it was he who taught the Indians the ways of civilized life and who led them to greater material prosperity and to increased contentment.

His widely heralded success and his model missionary life attracted other missionaries of note to this long neglected vineyard of the Lord. At the time of his coming, it had been a vast and trackless wilderness where, at times, no other voice but his proclaimed the true word of the true God. At his death there flourished a well established diocese with more than twenty priests and a number of churches, fitting memorials to his zeal and his industry.

He was grave, dignified, urbane, sincere and at all times a gentleman and a priest. He never paraded his knowledge in public nor boasted of his fame. Neither did he seek whatever glory the products of his industry and talents merited. Rich and poor, without respect to creed or color, whoever was fortunate enough to make his acquaintance, held him in high esteem.

Undoubtedly he made mistakes. But they were errors of judgment rather than errors of the heart, for he was human and as fallible as any other man. A close study of his life does not reveal a single blot to mar the purity of his soul. It stands revealed as a life that has been described as one of the jewels of our hierarchical crown. Even during his lifetime he was regarded by many as a saint. Many mementos of him have been preserved and cherished as precious heirlooms from generation to generation. Although he died more than sixty years ago, his memory is as fresh as if he had died but yesteryear. Time serves only to add luster to his fame and to blend his life into a harmonious whole.

God had shown special regard for this beloved servant of His by protecting and strengthening him on his perilous and wearisome missionary journeys. More than once the Master spared His faithful servant's life when that life was in extreme danger and death seemed almost certain. His unflinching trust in his God survived all perils; he died by the calm of his own fireside.

The people of Michigan have not forgotten this great hero nor the great service he has rendered them. They have named a county, a post-office and a state park after him. The city of Marquette has named one of its principal thoroughfares in his honor.

The study of his life should make our own faith more profound. It should create in us a desire to emulate his virtues. It should strengthen our own trust in God and turn our thoughts more to prayer. It should instill in our hearts a patriotic pride in this pioneer Catholic, the Apostle of the Chippewas, whose labors have been of inestimable value in the development of the country in the vicinity of Lake Superior. Let his name be revered, and may God grant that it may, some day, be enrolled canonically among those of His Saints.

BIBLIOGRAPHY

Armstrong, Benj. G.,
  "Early Indian History," Ashland, Wisconsin 1892

Ayer Collection, Newberry Libray, Chicago

Benkovic, Josip,
  "Irenej Friderik Baraga."
  Published in "Dom in Svet." Jugoslavia, 1897

Bren, Rev. Hugo, S.T.D., O.F.D.,
  "Baraga's Letters, Hitherto Unpublished."
  Translated from the German. Copies in his possession.
  Published in *Ave Maria,* a Slovene monthly magazine,
  Lemont, Illinois, 1930-1931

Jaklic, Rev. Franc, S.T.D.,
  "Friderik Baraga," Jugoslavia 1931

Notre Dame University, Archives

Rezek, Rr. Rev. Msgr. A. I., L.L.D.,
  "History of the Diocese of Sault Ste. Marie and Marquette,"
  Houghton, Michigan, 1906

Verwyst, Rev. Chrys., O.F.M.
  "Life and Labors of Bishop Baraga,"
  Milwaukee, Wisconsin, 1900

Voncina, Rev. Dr. Leon,
  "Friderik Baraga," Jugoslavia 1869 and 1906

Zaplotnik, Rev. J. L., J.C.D., V.F.
  "Additional Lights on the Life of Bishop Baraga."
  Published in *Ave Maria Almanac* (Slovene) 1930-1932,
  Lemont, Illinois.
  Also, "Lecture Delivered by Bishop Baraga, 1863."
  Published in *Acta et Dieta,* vol. V. p. 99-110,
  St. Paul, Minnesota, 1917

For more information on Bishop Baraga or to make a
contribution to support the cause for his canonization,
please contact:

Bishop Baraga Association
615 S. Fourth Street
Marquette Michigan 49855

(906) 227-9117

www.BishopBaraga.org

www.ingramcontent.com/pod-product-compliance
Lightning Source LLC
Chambersburg PA
CBHW052142150726

48002CB00003B/1031